ACT I

SCENE 1

The living-room of a ground-floor apartment in one of London's old houses, near Sloane Square. It is spring. Tuesday afternoon

It is a well-furnished, comfortable room, reflecting both the good taste and industry of a best-selling novelist. There are comfortable chairs, a sofa, drinks table, a filing cabinet, an antique chest of drawers, tables with lamps, etc. There is also a large desk on which are several unopened letters, a dictating machine, reference books, telephone, and an attractive lamp. A raised alcove, back C, is used as a dining area

A section of the hall can be seen leading, UR, to the front door. The kitchen and rear entrance to the flat are reached through a door DR. A second door, always kept open, UL, leads to the bedrooms, etc. A collection of leather-bound "Max Telligan" novels is on view in the room together with several signed photographs of well-known personalities

When the CURTAIN rises, Liz Ferber is at the desk, typing. From time to time she consults a notebook which contains handwritten notes. After a little while the front doorbell is heard

Liz rises and goes out into the hall

We hear the opening of the front door and the sound of voices

Liz (*off; surprised*) Why, hello, Harriet!
Harriet (*off*) Don't look so surprised, Liz! You make me feel I'm not welcome . . .
Liz (*off*) Of course you're welcome! Come along in!

Harriet Telligan enters with Liz. Harriet is an attractive, well-dressed woman who at this moment appears faintly agitated. Liz now carries a copy of the "Evening Standard" which she puts down on one of the tables

Harriet (*looking around the room*) Where's Max? Is he out?
Liz He's in Munich. I'm expecting him back this evening or tomorrow morning at the latest.
Harriet What on earth is he doing in Munich?
Liz He's meeting an American film producer who's interested in his latest book.
Harriet Well, let's hope he doesn't do to *Still Life* what that Italian producer did to *A View from the Patio*. It was disaster! The worst film I've ever seen.

Liz I never saw it. It was before I worked for Max. Are you staying in town, Harriet?

Harriet Yes, just for two or three nights. I shall be going back to Beaconsfield on Thursday. (*Taking an Inland Revenue envelope out of her handbag*) This arrived yesterday. I opened it by mistake. It's another tax demand.

Liz (*nodding*) I'll take care of it.

Harriet (*restlessly pacing the room*) Max has been living here for nearly two years, yet these wretched tax things still keep coming to the house! Why? You're his secretary, Liz. Can't you do something about it?

Liz The accountants have written to the Inland Revenue, more than once.

Harriet Well, tell them to write again!

Liz I'll see to it, Harriet. Now stop worrying!

Harriet (*turning; and relenting slightly*) I know I'm making a fuss, Liz. I just can't help it. I make a meal of everything these days. (*She moves down to the sofa*)

Liz Once the divorce has gone through you'll feel differently. Everything will be perfectly straightforward.

Harriet I doubt that. I doubt that very much. I saw my solicitor the other day . . .

Liz What did he have to say?

Harriet I went with a mass of questions and he didn't answer one of them. Just gave me a quiet little lecture. I sometimes wonder whose side he's on. (*A moment*) Liz, if I ask you something will you be perfectly frank with me?

Liz Oh, dear! Now what am I letting myself in for?

Harriet You're not letting yourself in for anything. Just be honest with me, that's all.

Liz All right. Fire ahead.

Harriet Would you say that I was a difficult person?

Liz (*after a brief pause; fencing*) No, no, I wouldn't say that you were . . . difficult . . .

Harriet Argumentative, perhaps?

Liz That's not a word I would use.

Harriet What word would you use?

Liz I'd say that you were inclined to be a little . . .

Harriet A little what?

Liz (*with a laugh; changing her mind*) Look, Harriet – I haven't known you very long, so it's impossible for me to answer your question. I can only say that I like you – and I like Max. And I'm very sorry that the pair of you split up. Why you split up, I don't know. And it's none of my business.

Harriet We just never stopped having arguments. We used to argue over the most ridiculous things. Quite absurd some of them. Towards the end almost everything sparked off a row of some kind. It's sad really, because I'm still very fond of Max . . .

Liz Harriet, do you know what I would do if I were you?

Harriet No. Tell me. What would you do?

A Touch of Danger

A Play

Francis Durbridge

Samuel French – London
New York – Sydney – Toronto – Hollywood

FOR AMATEUR PRODUCTION ENQUIRIES

UNITED KINGDOM AND WORLD EXCLUDING NORTH AMERICA

plays@samuelfrench.co.uk
020 7255 4302/01

Each title is subject to availability from Samuel French, depending upon country of performance.

A TOUCH OF DANGER

First produced at the Theatre Royal, Windsor, on 21st July, 1987. Subsequently presented in London by Bill Kenwright at the Whitehall Theatre, London, on 12th September, 1988, with the following cast of characters.

Liz Ferber	Virginia Stride
Harriet Telligan	Pauline Yates
Jeff Seago	Derren Nesbitt
Max Telligan	William Franklyn
Vincent Crane	Charles Rea
Lloyd Mitchell	Max Mason
Graham Digby	William Lucas
Connie Palmer	Cathy Flanagan
Rose	Sarah Beeson

The play directed by Mark Piper
Designed by John Page

The action of the play takes place in the living-room of Max Telligan's apartment near Sloane Square, London

ACT I   SCENE 1   Tuesday afternoon
        SCENE 2   Tuesday afternoon. Later
        SCENE 3   Tuesday night
        SCENE 4   Tuesday night. An hour later

ACT II SCENE 1   Tuesday night. Immediately after
        SCENE 2   Wednesday morning
        SCENE 3   Wednesday afternoon
        SCENE 4   Thursday morning

Time – the present

Liz I'd take a holiday. Go away for a couple of weeks and try and stop worrying about the divorce, about Max, about everything that's happened to you during the past two years.

Harriet (*shaking her head as she rises*) Would you now? And where would you go? Some exciting little health farm brimming over with yoghurt. It's no use, Liz. Going away wouldn't help. Not one little bit.

Liz How do you know it wouldn't?

Harriet Because I've been away. I had a short stay in the South of France. I only got back on Thursday.

Liz I didn't know that.

Harriet I didn't tell anyone I was going. Not even Marsha. She was staying with some friends in Ireland and I just didn't know what to do with myself.

Liz It's ages since I was in the South of France. Did you go on your own?

Harriet stares at her for a split second, obviously surprised by the question

Harriet Of course I went on my own! Who do you think I went with?

Liz I—I don't know, Harriet. I just wondered if you'd gone with a friend, that's all.

Harriet No, I didn't go with a friend. I was on my own. I'm on my own most of the time these days.

Liz You needn't be, Harriet. You're an attractive woman.

Harriet The holiday, if you can call it that, was a disaster. Utter disaster! Apart from everything else the weather was awful and the hotel was dreadful—full of the most frightful people. I just couldn't wait to get back to Beaconsfield. Anyway, I can't leave Marsha just now, even if I wanted to. She's just started a new job. I don't know whether Max told you, she's now in the book department at Harrods.

Liz Yes, he told me. Does she like it?

Harriet Enormously. She adores the job—but the silly girl's talking about moving into a place of her own. Which is quite ridiculous. She's far too young to leave home. Don't you agree, Liz?

Liz (*evasively*) Well—let's just say, I'm glad it's your problem, Harriet, and not mine.

Harriet You're just as bad as Max! He won't commit himself. I wrote him a letter about Marsha—must be over a fortnight ago—and I don't even know whether he read it.

Liz I'm sure he did.

Harriet glances across at the desk

Harriet What's he working on at the moment? (*She crosses and looks at the script in the typewriter*) I needn't have asked! The diary, of course! A couple of weeks ago I asked Max if he'd let me read it. What there is of it, so far. He refused.

Liz That doesn't surprise me. He won't let anyone see it, not until it's finished. And it's more than my job's worth to even talk about it, he's made that quite clear on more than one occasion. You've never stopped telling Max that he's wasting his time and ought to be writing another novel.

Harriet Liz, for heaven's sake, I was married to the man for nearly twenty years! I want to know what he's written about me!

Liz It so happens he's written some very nice things about you.

Harriet (*with a shrug*) Anyway, why should I worry? In spite of all the publicity it'll be a flop. People are only interested in novelists when they're dead. Although Marsha doesn't agree with me, of course. She thinks the diary will be a terrific success. But then she thinks everything her father does is terrific. (*She moves down to Liz, a puzzled expression on her face*) Liz, tell me: does the name Lloyd Mitchell mean anything to you?

Liz No. Should it?

Harriet He's an American and a great fan of Max's. At least, he says he is.

Liz We get lots of letters from the States. Lloyd Mitchell? . . . I don't recall the name . . .

Harriet He bought a copy of *Still Life* and got talking to Marsha about the book. It transpired he'd read practically everything Max had written. Marsha was highly amused and finally, of course, she told him who she was. He didn't believe her at first. Then, when he did believe her, she had great difficulty getting rid of him. (*A shade agitated*) It was very odd. He wanted to know about the diary. When he discovered she hadn't read any of it he simply bombarded her with a whole lot of other questions.

Liz Yes, well—there's a perfectly simple explanation. He's not just a fan, he's from a newspaper or one of the magazines. It's the usual ploy. Marsha gave him an interview without realizing it. I know those people! They're the same the world over!

Harriet (*not convinced*) You could be right. It's just that I find it strange that he should have asked so many questions. (*She hesitates, then:*) Well—I mustn't keep you any longer. When you see Max tell him I called . . . (*She moves towards the hall*)

Liz Yes, of course, Harriet.

Harriet I must talk to him about Marsha. I really must. Perhaps you'll tell him that?

Liz Yes, I'll tell him.

Harriet (*after a slight hesitation, as if wishing to prolong the conversation*) Well—I'll be off.

Harriet goes out to the hall

Pause. Liz picks up her notebook and is about to return to the typewriter, when . . .

Harriet re-appears with Jeff Seago. He is a well-built man in his late thirties

You've got a visitor, Liz.

Liz (*surprised*) Why, hello, Jeff! What are you doing in town? (*She rises and joins Jeff and Harriet*)

Jeff I had a luncheon date and drank too much. So I thought I'd better take the rest of the day off. No use telling someone to keep their eye on the ball if you can't see it yourself! Is Max around?

Liz No, I'm afraid he isn't. He's away at the moment.
Jeff Ah, well! Not to worry. Some other time.

He suddenly realizes that Harriet is staring at him

Liz Oh, I'm sorry. Do you know Mrs Telligan?
Jeff (*turning towards Harriet*) Jeff Seago, Mrs Telligan. (*After a small pause*) I'm the golf professional at Midway Park.
Harriet Yes, of course! How stupid of me! I thought I recognized you.
Jeff You came to the club several times, to pick up Max.
Harriet Yes, I remember.
Liz Is there anything I can do, Jeff?
Jeff Well—as a matter of fact . . . I was going to ask Max for a signed copy of one of his books. It's for my nephew, it's his birthday on Sunday.
Liz Oh, I see. Leave it with me. What do they call your nephew?
Jeff Robert . . .

Liz returns to the desk and picking up a pen makes a note of the name on a pad

Harriet How old is he?
Jeff He'll be sixteen. Books—books—books—he thinks of nothing else. Golf, he just doesn't want to know! (*To Liz*) I've been shooting a line about Max, so I know he'd be thrilled to get a signed copy of one of his novels.
Liz No problem, I'm sure.

Pause

Jeff Do you play golf, Mrs Telligan?
Harriet No, I'm afraid I don't.
Jeff You should. You've got the build for it.
Harriet (*none too happy with the remark*) Thank you. That's nice to know.
Jeff If you ever feel like taking it up, please don't hesitate to get in touch with me. I'd be delighted to give you a few lessons.
Harriet You're very kind.
Liz Yes, well—take my tip, think twice, Harriet! He once talked me into having a lesson and we spent most of the time in a bunker. It took me a week to get the sand out of my hair!
Jeff (*laughing*) You gave up too soon, Liz. That was your trouble. (*Turning towards the hall*) Remember me to Max.
Liz I'll do that. And I'll make sure you get the book.
Jeff Thank you. I appreciate it.

Jeff smiles at Harriet and, giving Liz a friendly nod, goes

Harriet moves down to Liz as the phone starts ringing

Harriet What did he mean, I've got the build for it?
Liz It was a compliment, Harriet.
Harriet You could have fooled me!
Liz (*picking up the phone*) Hello? . . . yes, it is . . . (*Surprised*) Oh, hello, Marsha! . . . Yes, your mother's here; we've just been talking about—— (*She stops; alarmed*) What is it? What's the matter, my dear?

Harriet instinctively moves nearer the phone

Why are you crying? . . . (*Staggered*) What!!! . . . Who told you? . . . When did you hear this? (*Softly*) Oh, my God!
Harriet What is it? What's happened?

Liz looks at Harriet, stunned

What is it, Liz?
Liz Max is dead . . .
Harriet (*aghast*) Dead? No, no, that can't be true!
Liz It was on the radio . . .

Harriet grabs hold of the phone

Harriet (*on the phone; tensely*) Marsha, are you sure about this? . . . When did you hear it? . . . Marsha, for God's sake stop crying! . . . Yes, I'm listening. . . . (*Long pause*) Yes, all right, my dear. . . . (*Quietly*) No, don't do that, I'll go straight back to the hotel and pack. . . . I'll see you later . . .

She replaces the phone and obviously badly shaken by the news, moves slowly down to Liz who has picked up the evening paper

Liz It's not in the paper . . .

Harriet slowly buries her head in her hands. Liz continues searching the paper

(*Suddenly*) Yes, here it is! It's in the stop-press . . .

Harriet looks up

(*Reading*) "Max Telligan, the well-known novelist, whose eagerly awaited diary is to be published next year, was found dead in a car on the outskirts of Munich in the early hours of this morning . . ."
Harriet In a car? Was it an accident?
Liz (*still staring at the paper*) I don't know . . . it doesn't say . . .

Harriet moves down to Liz and takes the newspaper from her. Pause

Harriet (*staring at the announcement; stunned*) "Found dead in a car on the outskirts of Munich . . ." I can't believe this! I just can't . . . What do you think happened, Liz?
Liz I don't know! But we'll find out! I'll phone the paper!

Liz takes the newspaper from Harriet and searches the paper for the telephone number. Eventually she finds it and quickly crosses to the phone. She dials. A long pause. The number is ringing out

(*On the phone; tense, keyed-up*) This is Liz Ferber, Max Telligan's secretary—please put me through to the news room. (*Pause*) This is Max Telligan's secretary . . . I've just seen your announcement in the stop-press and I'd be grateful if you could give me some further information. . . . Yes, but what happened, exactly? . . . Yes, I know! It says that in the paper! But *what happened?* (*Tense pause*) Yes, I'm listening. . . . I see. . . . That's very kind of you. Thank you . . . (*Liz slowly replaces the receiver*)

Harriet (*overwrought*) Is it true?

Liz (*her thoughts elsewhere*) Yes, it's true.

Harriet Well—what happened?

Liz (*hesitant, as if trying to make a decision*) They don't really know what happened . . .

Harriet Surely, they must know! Was it a car accident?

Liz It—it doesn't sound like it.

Harriet What do you mean, it doesn't sound like it? Liz, you're keeping something back from me!

Liz Harriet, wait! Please wait! Give me time to think! (*She finally reaches a decision and begins a frenzied search of the desk. She finally comes across a British Airways timetable. She consults the timetable, at last finding the details she is looking for*) There's a British Airways flight to Munich at sixteen-twenty! Can you make it?

Harriet Yes. I—I think so . . .

Liz Go back to the house as soon as you can and pick up your passport. I'll arrange for the tickets . . .

As Liz speaks we hear the noisy opening and closing of the front door. Both Liz and Harriet turn towards the hall

Max Telligan enters. He is a distinguished looking man, casually dressed. He carries a suitcase and a large parcel. He stops in his tracks, both surprised to see Harriet and the expression on Liz's face

Harriet Max!

Max What is this? What's going on? (*He puts down the suitcase and parcel*) Has something happened?

Liz hands him the newsaper. A tense pause, whilst Max reads the stop-press announcement

How on earth did they get hold of this story?

Black-out

SCENE 2

The same. Late Tuesday afternoon

Liz is sitting at the desk talking to someone on the telephone

Liz (*on the phone*) . . . Yes, of course I will, Samantha. Not to worry, I'll take care of it. What is it this time, a mink coat? . . . Yes, I promise . . . Yes, I will . . . No problem, no problem at all . . . (*She replaces the receiver*)

Max enters from the bedroom

Max Isn't it time you left, Liz?

Liz Yes, I'm just off.

Max Who was that on the phone? Another newspaper?

Liz (*with a gesture towards the ceiling*) No, it was the young lady upstairs.

She's expecting an important parcel tomorrow morning and she's going to be out all day. I said we'd take care of it for her . . .

Max (*moving down to the desk*) You know, this is getting out of hand, Liz! If it isn't parcels it's flowers!

Liz Yes, but she's always terribly grateful, Max. And she did give you some after-shave, remember.

Max You don't have to remind me! I came out in a rash!

Liz picks up a folder and a notebook

Liz I've finished the typing.

Max Oh good. (*He takes the folder from her. He looks at the contents of the folder*)

Liz Only four split infinitives this time.

Pause. Max continues reading the manuscript, turning over the pages. He finally closes the folder

Max We'll go through this tomorrow. What about the material I dictated over the phone?

Liz I think I got most of it, but it wasn't a particularly good line. (*She consults her notebook*) Would you like me to read part of it?

Max If you've got time.

A tiny pause; whilst Liz studies her notes, then:

Liz (*reading*) "April thirtieth, Munich. Terry Wilde arrived this evening — shortly before six o'clock, and just when I was beginning to think he wasn't going to turn up after all. It's pretty warm here, for the time of the year, but that hasn't stopped our Terry from wearing a fur hat and what appears to be a mink-lined anorak. It must be seven or eight years since we last met, but he hasn't changed a great deal. He still calls me Max with monotonous regularity . . ."

Max Tex! He still calls me *Tex* with monotonous regularity . . .

Liz Oh! (*She smiles and makes the alteration in her notebook*)

Max Thank you, Liz.

Liz rises and, preparing to leave, gathers up her handbag, etc., from the desk

Liz What finally happened in Munich? Is Terry Wilde going to buy *Still Life*?

Max (*after a moment*) No.

Liz (*surprised*) He's not?

Max No. He's not interested in the book. I doubt whether he's even read it.

Liz Then why the meeting? What was it all about?

Max hesitates, then looks at her. A tiny pause

Max He wants to buy the diary.

Liz (*astonished*) The diary?

Max Yes.

Liz You mean——(*Puzzled*) How on earth can he make a movie out of the diary?

Max He doesn't want to make a movie out of it. He's not in the film business, not any longer. He's in publishing.

Liz But you're under contract to Cromwell House ...

Max Only for novels. Wilde's made me a fantastic offer, Liz. For the life of me I just don't see how I can turn it down. (*A moment*) He wants to buy the diary outright and he's offered me a million dollars.

Liz (*thunderstruck*) A million dollars!

Max Yes. For the world rights.

Liz You're joking!

Max No, I'm not joking.

Liz A million dollars! The man's crazy!

Max He may be crazy, but he's serious. Dead serious. He's coming to London next week and we're going to discuss it further.

As Liz shakes her head in apparent disapproval

How can I refuse this sort of an offer? Apart from solving the tax stituation, it just wouldn't be fair to either Harriet or Marsha if I turned it down.

Liz (*after a tiny pause*) Incidentally, Marsha came to see me.

Max Marsha did? When?

Liz A couple of days ago. She wants to share a flat with a girl friend. They've seen a place they like in Holland Park and Marsha asked me to talk to you about it.

Max Yes, Harriet's been on about this for some time. She's against the idea.

Liz And you?

Max Frankly, I don't know whether I'm against it or not. (*A moment*) I suppose Marsha would be better sharing a flat with someone, rather than taking a place of her own — which is what she's been talking about during the past six months.

Liz Yes, well, it's not for me to take sides, but — Marsha told me she hasn't been getting on at all well with her mother just recently ...

Max I know, and I've been worried about it. (*After a tiny pause*) I'll talk to Marsha. She's staying here at the weekend.

Liz There's been another tax demand, by the way. I've sent it to the accountants. They want to see you. I've made an appcintment for five o'clock tomorrow.

Max nods

Liz Harriet's been away, she went down to the South of France for a few days.

Max (*surprised*) I didn't know that.

Liz It was while Marsha was in Ireland. It was a disaster, I'm afraid. The weather wasn't good and she hated the hotel she was staying in.

Max And everyone in it, I'll bet.

Liz (*moving towards the hall*) I doubt whether I'll be in before tomorrow afternoon, Max. I have a dentist appointment in the morning and I'm not sure how long it will take. Or what I'll be feeling like!

Max Not to worry. If you don't feel like coming in give me a ring.

As Liz is about to go she notices a very attractive clock on one of the tables

Liz That clock's new . . .
Max Yes.
Liz Did you buy it in Munich?
Max I didn't buy it at all. It's a present for Marsha from Terry Wilde.

He joins Liz who is admiring the clock

I happened to tell him that Marsha was hoping to move into a place of her own one day and the next morning he handed me this and said, "Give this to your daughter—it's for the flat."
Liz It's a lovely clock.
Max I was quite embarrassed. (*With a shake of the head*) Terry's an extraordinary chap, he really is! He'll argue like the devil over the price of a cup of coffee—then he'll do this sort of thing.
Liz It must have cost the earth. (*She turns towards the hall again, then hesitates*) When you next see Harriet, try and be nice to her. She really is worried about Marsha. Teenage daughters aren't easy to deal with.
Max (*a shade querulous*) I'm acutely aware of that . . .
Liz I'm sorry, Max, I didn't mean to . . . (*With an uneasy little laugh*) One of these days you'll tell me to mind my own business.
Max (*regretting his reaction*) I daren't, you might walk out on me. Then I'd have nothing left—except my split infinitives.

Liz laughs and exits

Max turns his attention to several letters on the desk. He is about to read one of them when voices are heard in the hall

Liz returns with Vincent Crane. He wears a dark suit, carries a valise, and walks with the aid of a stick. His manner is pleasant if somewhat disarming

Liz (*puzzled*) There's someone to see you, Max.
Crane Mr Telligan?
Max (*putting the letter down*) Yes?
Crane I must apologize for dropping in like this, sir, without an appointment. But it is—rather important. My name is Crane. Vincent Crane.
Max (*none too friendly*) Yes Mr Crane?
Crane I think we have a mutual friend at Scotland Yard, sir? Chief Superintendent Hamley.
Max Dave Hamley?
Crane That's right. He wishes to be remembered to you.
Max (*after a moment*) Thank you, Liz.

Liz goes

Max How is Dave?
Crane He's well, but unfortunately he gets very little time for squash these days. Which doesn't please him, I'm afraid. I gather that's how you met, sir?

Max Yes, at the RAC club. He beat the living daylight out of me.

Crane Well—I'm certainly delighted to meet you, Mr Telligan. I've always enjoyed your books. Especially *A View from the Patio*.

Max Thank you.

Crane I'm afraid I haven't got round to reading *Still Life* yet . . .

Max I trust you will. (*A moment*) Why did you wish to see me?

Crane (*hesitantly*) I wonder—may I sit down, sir?

Max Yes, of course. I'm sorry.

Crane looks at the sofa, then at the chairs. He finally decides on one of the armchairs

Crane (*indicating his ankle*) My wife's a keep-fit fanatic. The other morning, when she was doing her exercises, I said any damn fool can do that sort of thing. (*As he lowers himself into the chair*) Alas, this fool couldn't . . .

Max smiles and sits on the arm of the sofa

Max Are you a colleague of Superintendent Hamley's?

Crane Yes, I am. (*He takes out his wallet and displays a CID identity card*) We used to share the same office, but about a year ago he was assigned to special duties—whatever that may mean!—so we see very little of each other these days, unfortunately. (*Replacing his wallet*) Mr Telligan, I'm making inquiries about a friend of yours and I'd be grateful, most grateful, sir, if you'd answer a few questions . . .

Max A friend of mine?

Crane A man called Terry Wilde.

Max (*surprised*) Terry Wilde?

Crane Yes, I understand you saw him, quite recently, in Munich?

Max Yes, I saw him. But why are you interested in Mr Wilde?

Crane (*ignoring the question*) I'd like you to tell me a little bit about the gentleman, sir. Amongst other things, how you came to meet him in the first place—and why you had dinner with him at the Vier Jahreszeiten?

Max (*a momentary hesitation; his curiosity managing to control a slight irritation*) I first met Terry Wilde about seven or eight years ago when he was making a film at Pinewood Studios. Last week my agent telephoned me and said that Terry had read *Still Life*, was interested in the film rights, and wanted to see me . . .

Crane Go on, sir . . .

Max I flew to Munich and, as you quite rightly say, had dinner with him. During the course of the meal I discovered my agent had got it all wrong—or Terry had misled him. He wasn't interested in making a film. He simply wanted to buy the rights in a diary I've been keeping over the years.

Crane Did he make an offer for the diary, sir?

Max Yes he did. A fantastic offer.

Crane (*after a moment*) Was anyone else present when you had dinner with Mr Wilde?

Max No. No-one. Why do you ask?

Crane (*ignoring the question*) Did you see Mr Wilde again, sir, before leaving Munich?

Max Yes, he came to my room this morning, just as I was leaving for the airport. He had a present for my daughter.

Crane A present for your daughter?

Max Yes.

Crane (*after a thoughtful pause; reaching for his stick*) Well—thank you, sir. I won't take up any more of your valuable time. You've been most helpful.

They both rise

Max Have I? Well—I'm glad you think so. And now, may I make a suggestion?

Crane Of course, by all means . . .

Max Since you're quite obviously interested in Mr Wilde and his activities, to say nothing of his friends, don't you think it might be a good idea if you addressed some of your questions to Mr Wilde himself, rather than to me?

Crane Under the circumstances that might prove to be a little difficult, sir.

Max What circumstances?

Crane He's dead.

Max (*stunned*) Dead!

Crane His body was found in a car, early this morning on the outskirts of Munich. He'd been shot between the eyes. Several times . . .

Max (*suddenly, staring at Crane in amazement*) Near Munich?

Crane That's right. The car in question was rented. The police found a copy of the rental agreement in the glove pocket. The agreement had your name on it, Mr Telligan, and was signed by you. (*A watchful pause*) Can you account for that, sir?

Max Yes, I can! I rented the car on arrival in Munich but this morning I was pushed for time so I decided to take a cab to the airport. Terry offered to return the car to Hertz for me, so I gave him the key.

Crane (*after a moment*) It's as simple as that?

Max Yes, it's as simple as that. (*Still stunned, more or less under his breath*) Terry Wilde murdered . . . I—I just can't believe it . . .

Crane It's true, sir. (*He moves slowly towards the hall, then hesitates*) You said just now that Mr Wilde gave you a present, for your daughter?

Max hardly hears him, he appears greatly puzzled, his thoughts elsewhere

Max Yes . . .

Crane Have you delivered the present, sir?

Max (*after a moment, realizing what Crane has said*) No, not yet. (*He indicates the clock*) It's over there . . .

Crane (*surprised*) The clock?

Max Yes.

Crane crosses to the table. He stands looking at the clock. Pause

Crane How old is your daughter, sir?

Max How old? She's seventeen. She'll be eighteen next month. Why do you ask?

Crane It seems a curious present for a young lady. (*His eyes are still on the clock, admiring it. Slowly; a shade hesitantly*) I wonder—if I could ask a favour of you, Mr Telligan?

Max It depends. What is it you want?

Crane I'd rather like to borrow this clock, if I may?

Max (*surprised*) Borrow it? Why do you wish to borrow it?

Crane I'd very much like a colleague of mine to take a look at it. But I shall quite understand if you don't wish to part with it, sir.

Max What is it you're looking for, Mr Crane?

Crane (*after a moment*) We'll take great care of the clock, I assure you.

Max You haven't answered my question. What is it you're looking for?

They take each other in

Crane (*still ignoring the question*) The clock won't be tampered with in any way, and it'll be returned to you this evening, without fail, I promise you.

Another pause. Max is hesitating, undecided—finally he crosses to the desk and produces a large carrier from one of the drawers. He brings the carrier down to the table, picks up the clock and carefully places it in the carrier

Thank you, Mr Telligan. (*Taking the carrier*) That's very kind of you. You've been most co-operative, and I appreciate it.

He gives a friendly nod and exits

Max stands looking towards the hall, a strange, puzzled look on his face—then he suddenly makes a decision and crosses to the phone. He dials. Pause

Max (*on the phone*) Could I speak to Superintendent Hamley? . . . My name is Telligan. . . . Thank you. . . . Hello? . . . Dave? . . . Yes, it's Max! . . . That's right, but it wasn't George Washington it was Mark Twain. . . . Dave, I've just had a visit from a colleague of yours—Vincent Crane. . . . Yes, he told me you'd once shared an office. . . . Did you? Now that's interesting. . . . (*After a moment; curious*) Yes, but who is he, exactly? . . . The anti-terrorist branch? . . . Oh—oh, I see! . . . I haven't the slightest idea, Dave, except that he took away a clock which was intended for my daughter. . . . Look—why don't you drop in for a drink one evening and I'll tell you all about it? (*Another pause, then:*) Yes, please do that, I'd very much like to see you again. . . . Thank you, Dave . . .

Max replaces the receiver and stands for a moment deep in thought, then he walks towards the bedroom—as he does so the doorbell rings. He turns; looks towards the hall. A slight pause. The doorbell rings again. He hesitates, then as he crosses into the hall the bell is heard again, loud and insistent

We hear the opening and closing of the front door, followed by Harriet's voice

Harriet (*off*) Didn't you hear the bell the first time?

Max (*off*) I'm sorry, Harriet. If I'd known it was you I'd have jumped to it. You're the very last person I would want to keep waiting.

Max enters followed by his wife

Harriet Have you discovered how the papers got hold of that extraordinary story about your being found dead?

Max Yes, I have. A man called Terry Wilde was murdered. They found his body in a car which, it so happens, was rented by me. The documents were in my name.

Harriet Who told you this? Who told you the dead man was Wilde? It's not in any of today's papers.

Max I've had a visitor, from Scotland Yard. A friend of Dave Hamley's. He put me in the picture.

Harriet Well, I must say, I find this quite extraordinary!

Max gives a little sigh as he crosses to the sofa

Max (*sitting*) Yes, I thought you would. After you left here I said to myself, "One thing's for sure, Harriet's going to find this quite extraordinary."

Harriet Oh, dear! What have I let myself in for? You're in one of those moods, are you?

Max What mood would you like me to be in? I have a large selection to choose from these days.

Harriet I'll bet you have! (*She sits in one of the armchairs, at the same time indicating the typewriter on the desk*) I gather you're still wasting your time on the diary.

Max Yes, Harriet.

Harriet You're a fool. You should be writing another novel. For goodness sake, Max, come to your senses! The public aren't going to get excited over *your* diary! Who cares whether you had lunch with the Prime Minister? Who cares whether you were very nearly killed in a typhoon?

Max Monsoon, Harriet.

Pause

Harriet I take it you got my letter?

Max Yes, I got it.

Harriet Did you read it?

Max Of course I read it!

Harriet Why of course? I'm quite sure most of my letters find their way into your waste-paper basket.

Max Harriet, I'm tired and I've several things I must see to, so I'd be grateful if you'd get to the point. Why did you come here?

Harriet You know perfectly well why I came! I'm worried about Marsha and this friend of hers . . .

Max stares at her for a moment, trying hard to suppress his irritation

I really am worried, Max.

Max You don't like her friend, is that it?

Harriet I haven't said I don't like her.

Max Your letter gave me that impression.

Harriet As a matter of fact I was quite fond of the girl until there was all this talk about her sharing a flat with Marsha.

Max But Marsha's never stopped talking about having a place of her own. You know that. Surely it would be better for her to share with someone?

Harriet I thought you'd say that. I thought you'd side with your daughter!

Max I'm not siding with her! Why do you always pick a quarrel with me about Marsha? Surely to God you must realize by now that's why I walked out on you! I just couldn't take any more of it!

Harriet (*softly*) I'm devoted to my daughter . . .

Max Of course you are! We both are! But why do we have to quarrel about her the whole time? (*A moment*) What's your objection to Marsha sharing a flat with a girl friend?

Harriet What's my objection? (*With a kind of ironic bitterness*) Max, you never fail to surprise me! You must have written twenty novels, yet there are times when you're utterly and completely devoid of imagination! (*Scathingly*) Don't you realize what's happened to my life since you walked out on me? Don't you realize how much I depend on Marsha? How lonely I'd be without her?

Max (*a trace of guilt in his voice*) That's nonsense, Harriet, and you know it. You have a large circle of friends.

Harriet (*angrily*) WE had a large circle of friends! How many times do you think I've been invited out to dinner during the past eighteen months?

Max I don't know, Harriet. I really haven't the slightest idea.

Harriet Twice. Once by the doctor and his wife and once by that randy little bank manager.

Max gives a slightly embarrassed little shrug and looks away from her. There is a long, uncomfortable silence

(*Hesitating*) I — I saw the car the other day.

Max (*turning*) The car?

Harriet Our car. (*She looks at him*) The Volvo . . .

Max Oh! Are you sure?

Harriet I'm quite sure. NPE two-eight-four L.

Pause

Max Where did you see it?

Harriet It was on a meter near Peter Jones.

Pause

Max It must be ten years old.

Harriet Older than that surely? Marsha couldn't have been more than five or six when you bought it. It now belongs to a little man called Wadilove. He has an art gallery in Pimlico.

Max How do you know?

Harriet I was taking a good look at the inside of the car when he suddenly arrived carrying a picture.

Max (*shaking his head*) Fantastic car! Did you tell him we once owned it?

Harriet Yes, I told him. He was very sweet. Except that he tried to sell me the picture. (*A small pause*) I was dying to ask him if he'd done anything about the heater. We just never stopped arguing over that wretched heater! Did we, Max?

Max I seem to recall you mentioned it from time to time.

Harriet (*after a moment; hesitating*) Later, when I was having a coffee on my own, I realized how silly I'd been.

Max Silly?

Harriet Getting sentimental about a car, for God's sake!

Max (*with a peculiar intensity*) Why shouldn't you get sentimental about a car? We had some marvellous times in that Volvo. It was like parting with a dog when I sold it. (*A moment*) Why are you smiling?

Harriet You never liked dogs.

A strained silence, then Max rises

Max I'll talk to Marsha. I shall be seeing her at the weekend, she's staying here.

Harriet Yes, I know. It was my idea. (*Getting up*) She's going to a party in Chelsea and I didn't want some young fool driving her back to Beaconsfield.

Max Unfortunately I shan't be here on Saturday. I've got to go to Birmingham. I'll be back on Sunday morning. (*He takes a key out of his pocket*) You'd better give her this key—and tell her to take care of it, she very nearly lost it the last time she stayed here.

Harriet takes the key and puts it in her handbag

Harriet You're always off somewhere. What are you up to in Birmingham, signing copies of *Still Life*?

Max (*nodding*) It's one of those promotion dinners. The publishers insist on my being there. They're nearly always a crashing bore. (*A slight pause. Not unfriendly*) Harriet, I really have a hundred and one things to see to. So if you'll excuse me ...

Harriet makes no comment, but crosses towards the hall

Are you driving back to Beaconsfield?

Harriet No, I'm staying in Town for a couple of nights. I'm on one of those shopping sprees we always used to quarrel about. (*She pauses. Anxiously*) What are you going to do, Max?

Max (*not looking at her*) Do?

Harriet About Marsha and this friend of hers?

Pause

You've just got to do something!

Pause

(*Exasperated*) Max, please tell me! What do you intend to do?

He finally looks at her again, having made his mind up

Max I shall tell Marsha I don't approve of her sharing a flat with anyone at the moment and that, financially, it's just not on.

Harriet is agreeably surprised

Harriet Do you mean that?
Max Yes, I mean it.

She is about to say something, then suddenly changes her mind, and exits

Max, a shade weary, but somewhat relieved that the interview is over, goes into the bedroom

A long pause, then—the kitchen door opens and Lloyd Mitchell enters. He is a good-looking, self-possessed American. He carries a wallet-style case. After quietly taking stock of his surroundings he crosses the room and—believing the flat to be unoccupied—proceeds to search the desk. Pause. Lloyd obviously fails to find what he is looking for and, after surveying the room again, he picks up his case and moves down to the chest of drawers. He places his case on top of the chest and examines the drawers, which he discovers are unlocked. He is just about to search the chest when, to his astonishment, he hears a noise in the bedroom. Pause. Lloyd, curious, moves towards the door R. Suddenly—he freezes

Max enters. He stares at Lloyd in amazement

Who the hell are you? What are you doing here?
Lloyd (*smiling; full of apologies*) I'm sorry. I guess I've made a mistake. Obviously, I'm in the wrong apartment.
Max What is it you're looking for?
Lloyd (*pleasantly*) A friend of mine invited me round for a drink. Your door was open and I took it for granted this was his apartment.
Max (*aggressively*) That's nonsense! Complete nonsense! You haven't made a mistake and the door wasn't open! Now what are you doing here? What is it you want?

Lloyd's friendly expression changes

Lloyd I've already answered your question. (*He moves towards the hall*)
Max You've been searching for something! What is it? What are you after?
Lloyd I've explained the situation to you.
Max You've done nothing of the sort! Now tell me! How did you get in here? I want to know! And don't insult my intelligence with that story about a friend of yours and the door being open.

Silence

Did someone give you a key?

Lloyd doesn't answer

Well—did they?
Lloyd (*quietly*) A key wasn't necessary. Doors are never a problem.

Pause. Max is studying Lloyd

Max Who are you, exactly?

Lloyd makes no comment

You're an American, unless I'm mistaken.

Still no comment from Lloyd

I take it, you thought the flat was empty?

After a momentary hesitation Lloyd gives a little nod

Lloyd I was under the impression you had an appointment with your agent this afternoon.
Max I had, but it was cancelled. You appear to be well informed about my affairs.
Lloyd Obviously, not as well as I might be.
Max Well—since I'm not with my agent the best thing you can do is tell me what you're doing here, and what it is you're looking for.

Lloyd gazes at Max tolerantly sizing him up

Lloyd Don't you know what I'm looking for?
Max No, I don't.
Lloyd I'm looking for the calculator.
Max The calculator?
Lloyd The one Terry Wilde gave you.
Max (*shaking his head*) I don't know what you're talking about! The only thing Terry Wilde gave me was a clock.
Lloyd (*equally puzzled*) A clock?
Max Yes. It was a present for my daughter. I know nothing about a calculator.

Lloyd gives him a long, searching look

Lloyd I hope you're telling me the truth, Mr Telligan.
Max Of course I'm telling you the truth! Why should I lie to you? In any case, I never use a calculator—and even if I did, why should Terry Wilde give me one? (*With authority*) Now, perhaps you'll be good enough to tell me who you are and what this is all about?

Lloyd hesitates: it would appear that he is about to satisfy Max's curiosity, then he quickly changes his mind

Lloyd Some other time. Some other time, my friend.

The American moves, as if to leave, and Max impulsively grabs his arm in an attempt to detain him

Max To hell with that! Tell me now! I want to know!

Lloyd is surprised by the action and suddenly angry. A struggle develops. Then, with a swift, professional movement he releases himself and expertly throws Max across the back of the sofa and on to the floor

Lloyd quickly exits

It is several seconds before Max recovers. Distinctly angry with himself, he makes his way towards the drinks table. He has almost reached it when he notices Lloyd's case on top of the chest. He crosses to the chest, picks up the case, and carries it down to the desk. Max stands staring at the case, turning it over in his hands, obviously surprised by the weight. Finally, he zips it open and takes out a gun: a Smith and Wesson .38. He is staring at the gun in astonishment . . .

Black-out

SCENE 3

The same. Several hours later

Max enters from the hall with Crane

Max I must have had every newspaper in Fleet Street on the phone since you left. To say nothing of the German press . . .

Crane Yes, well--that was rather to be expected, I'm afraid.

Max looks at the carrier Crane is carrying

Max Well—did you examine the clock? Did you find what you were looking for?

Crane No, alas, I'm afraid we didn't. But thank you again for letting us take a look at it.

Crane hands Max the carrier and murmurs "Do you mind, sir?" as he puts his stick down and sits in one of the armchairs

You say the German newspapers have been on to you?

Max nods

What did they have to say?

Max They confirmed what you'd already told me about the car, and they wanted to know what I was doing in Munich. What Terry Wilde and I talked about.

Crane Did you tell them?

Max puts the carrier down

Max I simply said he'd read most of my books and was interested in my work generally.

Crane I see. (*He pauses*) Apart from the clock, Mr Telligan, did Terry Wilde give you anything else whilst you were in Munich?

Max No.

Crane He didn't ask you to deliver a package, or a letter perhaps, to a friend of his?

Max No he didn't.

Pause

Crane As I understand it, Mr Wilde gave you the clock just before you left for the airport?

Max Yes, he did.

Crane Were you already packed?

Max Yes—well, partly . . .

Crane Where was your suitcase, sir, can you remember?

Max It was on the bed.

Crane Was it open?

Max (*thoughtfully*) Yes, I think so.

Another pause

Crane Did you, by any chance, leave Mr Wilde alone in the room, with the suitcase?

Max No, I don't think—yes, I did, now you come to mention it. I went into the bathroom. (*Puzzled*) What are you suggesting? That Terry put something in the case whilst I was out of the room?

Crane I'm not suggesting anything, sir, only . . . Have you unpacked your case?

Max Not completely.

Crane Would you mind doing so, while I'm here?

Max looks at Crane for a long moment, then he picks up the carrier and walks quickly into the bedroom

A pause—during which Crane quietly takes stock of his surroundings

Max returns with the suitcase which he places on the sofa

Max Perhaps you'd like to search the case yourself?

Crane No, please. Go ahead.

Max opens the case and takes out numerous articles of clothing, also a pair of slippers, a dressing gown, a toilet bag, and a book. Then suddenly, and to his surprise, he comes across a medium-sized calculator which is in the pocket of a jacket. Pause. Crane rises, picks up his stick, and stares across at Max who is examining the calculator. Pause

It's not yours?

Max (*shaking his head*) No, it's not mine.

Crane Then what's it doing in your case?

Max (*puzzled*) I don't know . . . I can't imagine . . . (*Still looking at the calculator, he moves towards the desk*)

Crane joins him. Pause. They are both staring at the calculator

Crane If you've no objection, Mr Telligan, I'd like a colleague of mine to take a look at this calculator.

Max (*looking up*) The man who examined the clock?

Crane Yes, sir.

Max I've no objection, except that . . . (*He hesitates*)

Crane Except what, sir?

Max Except that I'd like to know what it is you're looking for.

Crane (*pleasantly*) Yes, I imagine you would, sir. Unfortunately, I can't answer that question.,

Max Can't? Or won't?

Crane I'd like to satisfy your curiosity. I really would—because you've been most co-operative. (*Smiling*) And heaven only knows you must have a hundred and one questions you'd like to ask me.

Max (*shaking his head*) To be frank, I've really only one question I'd like to ask you, Mr Crane.

Crane Only one? Well, I must say, if I were in your shoes I'd be bursting with curiosity.

Max After you left here with the clock, I telephoned our mutual friend Dave Hamley. I said "Dave, who is this chap Crane? What does he do exactly?"

Crane And what did Dave say?

Max Not a lot, I'm afraid. He was rather cagey.

Crane (*laughing*) Yes, that sounds like Dave.

Max But he did make one, rather interesting, observation—which brings me to my question. (*Looking at Crane's ankle*) How does a man in your condition manage to play squash?

Crane is startled, staring at him uneasily. Pause

It would appear that you are somewhat at a loss for an explanation.

Crane I'm at a loss, because I don't understand what you're getting at.

Max Don't you? It's really quite simple. Dave Hamley said he'd played a game of squash with you this morning.

Crane (*after an uncertain pause*) Well, obviously he was mistaken.

Max (*shaking his head*) What the Superintendent meant of course, was that he'd played squash with Vincent Crane. Not with you, my friend. (*Quietly*) Who are you? And why did you come here?

Another pause. Crane is eyeing him narrowly, stick in hand

Crane I think you know why I came. You have something, Mr Telligan. Something I want. I thought at first it was the clock, but I was mistaken. (*A moment*) Please give me the calculator.

Max makes no move

Max Why do you want what appears to be a perfectly ordinary calculator?

Crane I thought you only had the one question?

Max Curiosity is getting the better of me.

Crane Then you'd be well advised to curb your curiosity. Now please give me the calculator.

Pause. Max makes no attempt to hand over the calculator

(*With quiet authority*) Mr Telligan, I don't think you understand, let alone appreciate, exactly what's happened to you. By sheer accident, coincidence, call it what you will, you've become involved in a very dangerous situation. If you value your life, which I'm sure you do, you'll simply hand over that calculator and forget that I came here. That we ever set eyes on each other.

Max (*nervously clearing his throat*) If I value my life? Is that a threat?

Pause

Crane Did you ever, by any chance, read a book called *The Truth That Killed*?

Max Yes, I read it.

Crane Then no doubt you recall the Markov murder? The incident with the umbrella? (*He slowly raises the walking-stick, deliberately pointing it at Max. He no longer limps*)

Max (*frightened; staring at the stick*) Yes, I remember the Markov murder.

Crane Good. (*Moving the stick nearer Max as he advances towards him*) Then I don't have to explain what this is for. (*A tense pause*) I shall only have to touch you with it once, Mr Telligan. Just the once! But I'm sure you realize that. (*Quietly*) Now kindly pass me the calculator . . .

Max's eyes are fixed on the stick; which is dangerously near him. He hardly dare move. Finally, he hands Crane the calculator. Crane looks at the calculator and as he does so Max moves quickly away from him. Crane is suddenly aware of the movement. A tense moment, during which Max stares at the tip of the walking-stick.

Max You've got what you were looking for! Now, please go!

Crane Oh, no, Mr Telligan! It's not that simple. The moment I leave here, you'll start talking!

Max I won't, I promise you!

Crane And even if you don't talk, you'll write something in that diary of yours.

Max I shan't! That won't happen! I promise you . . .

Crane You won't be able to resist it, my friend!

Max backs away as Crane starts to close in on him again, the stick raised, poised to strike

Max For God's sake, don't be stupid! Why should I want to get further involved in something which doesn't concern me? I'm already out of my depth!

Crane You are indeed!

Crane moves swiftly forward and a terrified Max retreats further away from him, bumping into one of the armchairs. As Crane advances Max is unable to prevent himself from sinking into the chair. Crane is now standing over him, a threatening figure

Max Don't be a bloody fool! Put that stick down!

The stick is raised, ready to strike

(*Near desperation point*) Wait a minute! Just wait a minute! There's something I haven't told you! Something you ought to know . . .

Crane pauses; he is watching Max, highly suspicious

Crane What is it you haven't told me?

Max (*softly*) I lied to you.
Crane Lied to me? About what? When did you lie to me?

A tense pause

Max (*slowly; his eyes still on the stick*) The clock wasn't the only thing Terry
Wilde gave me.

Another pause

Crane What else did he give you?

Silence

Tell me!

*Pause. Max is hesitating. He gives the impression that, despite the desperate
situation he now finds himself in, he is not sure whether to confide in Crane or
not*

What else did Wilde give you?
Max Just as we were leaving the dining-room he suddenly took me on one
side and handed me a letter. It was marked confidential and addressed to
someone in Bristol. Terry said it was important that the letter be posted in
London.
Crane (*still suspicious; his eyes on Max*) So?
Max I said I'd post it for him the moment I got back.
Crane So?
Max Unfortunately there was a delay at Heathrow, which put me in rather
a bad mood, and I forgot all about it.
Crane You're bluffing, Mr Telligan! You're just playing for time!
Max (*shaking his head*) I've still got the letter. Whether you'll consider it
important or not . . . I just don't know . . . you must judge for yourself . . .

*Max has suddenly decided to take a gamble. Summoning up courage he rises,
turns his back on Crane, and crosses towards the filing cabinet. Crane, still
suspicious but nevertheless curious, follows him part of the way, then stops.
Max reaches the cabinet, hesitates, then unlocks one of the drawers. Again he
hesitates, then making a decision, he puts his hand in the drawer and suddenly
produces the Smith and Wesson .38*

*Immediately Crane sees the weapon he springs to the attack. Max fires the gun
just as he is about to be prodded with the walking-stick. Crane stares at Max,
hardly realizing what has happened—then stricken with pain and clutching his
chest he releases his hold on the stick and staggers across the room. Blood can
be seen pouring down the front of his shirt as he collapses near the sofa*

*Max is relieved, yet at the same time extremely frightened. After a tense
moment he puts the gun down and crosses to Crane—whose body is partly
hidden by the sofa. He appears distinctly shaken as he kneels down and
examines the dead man. A long pause—then Max slowly rises and returns to
the desk. He stands by the desk, undecided what to do next. Finally, he makes
a decision and picks up the phone. He dials 999—then almost immediately*

takes fright, changes his mind, and slams down the receiver. A pause. Max is staring across at Crane. He is still tense, still desperately worried, still uncertain of his next move. Then suddenly a possible plan of action occurs to him. After a nervous hesitation he picks up the phone again and dials

(*On the phone; trying to control the note of tenseness in his voice*) Is that the garage? . . . It's Mr Telligan, Reg . . . I want you to do me a favour. Would you be kind enough to bring the car round straightaway? . . . No, don't do that, just leave it in the mews. . . . There's no need – I've got a key. . . . Thank you. . . . I'll see you tomorrow morning. . . . Straightaway, Reg!

He slams the receiver down and goes quickly into the bedroom. After a pause, he re-enters carrying a dark sheet

He is about to cover the body with it when he notices Crane's walking-stick. He puts the sheet down, partly covering Crane, and crossing the room, gingerly picks up the stick. He contemplates it for a moment or two, then puts it down out of harm's way. As he does so his eye falls on the calculator, which is on the floor. He picks up the calculator and is examining it when the front doorbell rings. He freezes. Pause. The doorbell rings. Max gives a sharp intake of breath, his eyes on the hall. The bell rings again. Pause. The bell rings yet again. Suddenly it stops. A long silence – then with almost a sigh of relief Max once again gives the calculator his attention. He has finished his examination and is taking it down to the desk, when . . .

Harriet enters from the hall. She stops in her tracks, staring at the body

Max suddenly turns

Harriet!

Harriet (*still staring at Crane's body*) What happened! Who is this man?

Silence

Is he dead?

Max nods

But – but what happened? Did he break into the flat? (*She moves down to him*)
Max No, Harriet . . .
Harriet Then what's he doing here? Who is he, Max?
Max He came to see me about Terry Wilde. He told me he was a colleague of Superintendent Hamley's. When I telephoned Dave I discovered that wasn't true and that he . . . (*he hesitates; a note of panic in his voice*) . . . he tried to kill me, Harriet! I had no choice . . . there was nothing else I could do . . .
Harriet (*stunned*) What do you mean, nothing else you could do? (*She stares at him*) My God, Max! Are you telling me that *you* killed him?
Max I had to! . . . I had to defend myself! I had no choice! . . .

Harriet slowly turns and looks towards the sofa again

Harriet Why did he want to kill you?

Max (*desperately on edge*) I'm sorry, we can't talk! Not now!

Harriet Why did he come here? He must have had a reason? What is it he wanted from you?

Max (*stopping her*) Harriet, please! I've told you, we can't talk! Not now! I've got to have time to think. To decide what I'm going to do!

Harriet (*alarmed*) But there's only one thing you can do! You must send for the police and tell them what happened!

Max (*shaking his head*) They'd never believe me! They'd never believe my story!

Harriet But you've no alternative! Surely you realize that? (*A pause — staring at him*) You've got something else in mind! What is it? Tell me! (*Alarmed*) Tell me, Max!

Pause

Max I've sent for the car . . .

Harriet The car? Why?

Max Later tonight I'm . . . going to take him out to Hampstead Heath . . . and leave him there. (*Stopping a protest*) I know it's a risk! A terrible risk! But it's one I've got to take!

Harriet (*stunned*) You must be out of your mind! This isn't a novel, for God's sake! It's the real world! Don't you realize as soon as someone finds the body they'll contact the police! Within a matter of hours the police will——(*She stops*)

Pause

Max What is it? (*Staring at her*) What is it, Harriet?

Harriet (*after a tiny pause*) You said you'd spoken to Dave Hamley?

Max Yes.

Harriet What did you tell him?

Max I told him that someone called Crane had called here and that he'd . . . What are you thinking?

Harriet Have you got Dave's number?

Max I'm not sure. Why?

Harriet Phone him! Phone him immediately! Tell him Crane— or whatever his name is— tried to kill you and that you had to defend yourself. Explain exactly what happened . . .

As Max hesitates

You've got to do this, Max!

Max looks at her, then after a thoughtful pause, he crosses to the desk and consults his address/phone book. Pause

Have you got the number?

Max Yes, it's here . . . (*He hesitates*)

Harriet Then ring him, Max! Please . . .

Pause. Max still hesitates, then he picks up the phone and dials. Harriet moves down to him. A long pause

Max (*to Harriet; holding the phone*) There's no reply ... (*Then, just as he is about to put the phone down*) Dave! ... It's Max Telligan. ... Dave, that man I told you about, the man who came to see me. It wasn't Crane, he was an imposter. ... No, wait! Please wait, there's something I've got to tell you. (*A short pause, then*) He tried to kill me—he tried to kill me and in the end I had to defend myself. ... Yes ... yes, I did—that's exactly what happened—but I didn't intend to kill him! Believe me, I didn't! I was only trying to stop him from——... (*He stops; listens*) ... Yes, I'm listening. ... (*A significant pause*) I'm listening, Dave. ... No. ... No-one. ... (*He looks at Harriet*) I haven't seen or spoken to anyone. ... (*A long pause. He is listening intently to what Dave is saying*) I understand. ... Yes, I understand. ... I understand perfectly. ... Yes, I will. ... Thank you, Dave ... (*He replaces the receiver. The look on his face is one of bewilderment*)

Harriet (*with barely controlled anxiety*) What is it? What did he say?

Max He asked me if I'd contacted anyone. When I said I hadn't he told me to wait until ... (*Puzzled*) He said, "Do nothing, Max. Don't go to the door. Don't answer the phone ... A man called Digby will be with you in about forty minutes ..."

Harriet Digby?

Max (*deep in thought*) Yes ... (*Suddenly*) Harriet, you must go! I told Dave I hadn't spoken to anyone. If he finds out I've lied to him ...

Harriet I'll leave! But first, you've got to promise to phone me.

Max nods

I'm staying at the Basil Street Hotel.

Max I'll phone you as soon as I——(*He stops*) Wait a minute! (*A moment*) You know Campbell's, the wine bar, near Sloane Square?

Harriet nods

Go there—and wait for me. If it's at all possible, I'll join you. If not, I'll phone you later.

Harriet gives a tense nod and heads for the hall

Oh—and Harriet ...

She turns

(*Puzzled*) Why did you come back?

Harriet I wanted to thank you ...

Max Thank me?

Harriet For being so understanding ... about Marsha ...

Max Oh. Oh, I see.

They stand looking at each other, almost awkwardly

Then Harriet quickly exits

The Lights fade to a Blackout

SCENE 4

The same. An hour later

The body and walking-stick have been removed. Max is sitting on the sofa staring across at Graham Digby who is standing at the desk, phone in hand, dialling a number. His briefcase is on the desk near the calculator. Digby is in his early forties and could easily be mistaken for a Harley Street consultant

Digby (*on the phone; after a pause*) This is Digby. . . . They've just left. . . . No, we didn't use the ambulance after all. . . . It's the blue Mercedes. . . . They should be with you in about forty minutes. . . . Yes. . . . Yes, do that . . . (*He rings off, picks up the calculator and crosses down to Max*) I trust you've been impressed, Mr Telligan?

Max Yes, I'm impressed. (*He is still somewhat on edge, and is not quite sure what to make of Graham Digby or how to cope with him*) I'd be even more impressed if you'd tell me who you are, exactly?

Digby I thought I'd answered that question.

Max You simply told me that your name was Graham Digby and that you were a friend of Superintendent Hamley's.

Digby Well—for the moment, let's just say I'm concerned with Security, and leave it at that.

Max Security? That can mean a great many things these days.

Digby It can indeed. However I didn't come here to satisfy your curiosity. On the contrary, I came so you could satisfy mine. (*He pauses*) Why did you kill Rorke.

Max Rorke? Was that his name?

Digby So far as we know. It's certainly a name he used from time to time.

Max But I've told you why I killed him! I've told you more than once! Three times, if I remember correctly.

Digby (*unruffled*) I'm sure it is three times, Mr Telligan. You have an excellent memory. Which is precisely why I'd like to hear your story again. I have a horrible feeling I may have missed something.

Max I doubt it. I doubt it very much. (*A tiny pause, then*) After I'd given Crane—Rorke—the calculator . . .

Digby Call him Crane . . .

Max After I'd given him the calculator he went for me with the stick and I was terrified. Scared to death. Finally, I made out that Terry Wilde had handed me a letter. An important letter that had to be posted in London. I said I still had it—which wasn't true of course, there was no letter—but it enabled me to get to the file and reach for the gun.

Digby (*quietly*) And he fell for that?

Max Yes, he fell for it. (*A moment*) Crane wasn't bluffing. When your people examine the walking-stick they'll find a miniature cartridge gun concealed in the tip. It's charged with Ricin, the poison that killed Georgi Markov.

Pause

Digby Tell me a little more about the American. The man who, conveniently, left his gun behind.

Max (*still faintly on edge*) I've already told you what he looked like and what happened. There's nothing more I can add.

Pause

Digby He was looking for the calculator?

Max Yes.

Digby You're sure?

Max Of course I'm sure. He said so. He was under the impression Terry Wilde had given it to me.

Pause. Digby is examining the calculator

Digby You think this is all he wanted? The only reason he came here?

Max Why, yes . . .

Digby He didn't ask to see a copy of your diary, by any chance?

Max (*surprised by the question*) No, he didn't. And I certainly wouldn't have shown him a copy had he done so! But why would he want to see my diary?

Digby For the same reason that I'd like to see it, Mr Telligan. *(A tiny pause)* How many copies are there?

Max Three.

Digby And they're kept where?

Max I have a safe in the other room.

Digby (*with a little nod*) Perhaps you'd be good enough to get me a copy?

Max hesitates, as if about to refuse the request, then with a little nod, he exits L

Digby, left alone, takes the opportunity of taking a good look at the room; strolling around and examining the various objects and photographs. Eventually he reaches the desk and, after glancing at the various papers, etc., he notices Max's address/phone book. He picks up the book and is immediately interested in the list of names and telephone numbers. He looks towards the other room—wondering how long it will be before Max returns—then he crosses to his case, opens it, and takes out a small camera. He quickly returns to the desk and proceeds to photograph several pages of the phone book. Having completed this task he returns to the case, replaces the camera, and takes out a postcard-size photograph. He looks at the photograph before putting it in his pocket. He is casually strolling around the room again when . . .

Max returns carrying a large manuscript

Digby moves down to Max and takes the diary from him

Thank you. (*Looking at the manuscript*) How many people have read this, apart from yourself?

Max My secretary's read most of it. But there are one or two entries I've typed personally.

Digby Which no-one else has seen?

Max Yes.
Digby Why is that?
Max They're things I may wish to . . . change my mind about . . . at a later date . . .
Digby What sort of things?
Max References to various people. Relatives, friends, and the not so friendly . . .
Digby I see. (*A moment*) You didn't give Mr Wilde a copy to read?
Max No, I didn't. But we discussed it of course.
Digby After which he made you the fantastic offer?
Max Yes.
Digby (*smiling*) Which you took seriously?
Max (*puzzled, and somewhat irritated by Digby's smile*) Yes, which I took seriously.
Digby A million dollars is a great deal of money.
Max I'm aware of that.
Digby Did you get the impression he had that sort of loot?
Max How does one judge affluence these days? (*A shrug*) He was wearing a mink-lined anorak with Gucci written all over him, if that means anything.
Digby Is Terry Wilde mentioned in the diary?
Max He is now. There's a brief account of our meeting in Munich.
Digby But prior to that he wasn't mentioned?
Max (*giving the matter thought*) No, he wasn't.

Digby nods, crosses to the desk, puts the diary in his case and closes it. He returns to Max

Digby Mr Telligan, before I leave you, I have a photograph I'd like you to take a look at. (*He takes the photograph out of his pocket*) It shows two people sitting outside a café. We're pretty sure the man's Terry Wilde, but we're not absolutely certain. (*Handing Max the photograph*) Take a good look at it, and tell me what you think.

Pause. Digby watches him

Well?

Pause

Max Yes, it's Terry Wilde.
Digby You're sure?
Max I'm quite sure.

Max is still staring at the photograph. Digby still watching him

Digby You recognize the woman he's with, of course . . . ?

A long pause

Max Yes, I recognize her. It's my wife.

The Lights slowly fade

CURTAIN

ACT II

The same. The action is continuous

Max When was this photograph taken?
Digby About ten days ago.
Max Where?
Digby In the South of France. At Beaulieu-sur-Mer.

Pause. Max is still staring at the photograph, almost mesmerized by it

Max Who took the photograph?
Digby One of our people. A chap we call "Bikini". He has a boat down there. He spends his life taking photographs.

Pause

Max May I keep this?
Digby Yes, you may keep it. We have copies. I shall want to talk to you again, most probably tomorrow morning. What time does your secretary get here?
Max About ten.
Digby She lives in Town?
Max Yes. She has a flat quite near here.
Digby How long has Miss Ferber been with you?
Max Oh—getting on for two years now. My wife met her at some charity "do" or other, the Easter before last, and happened to mention that I was looking for a secretary.
Digby A lucky break for Miss Ferber.
Max It was a lucky break for both of us. She enjoys the work, we get on very well together, and she has a private income. Which means, unlike the previous young lady, we don't spend half the day talking about the cost of living.
Digby You say she usually arrives about ten?
Max Yes, but we have a very free and easy arrangement. As long as she gets through the work, I'm quite happy. She's not coming in at all tomorrow morning. She has a dentist's appointment.
Digby Good! (*He crosses to the door* R) I'll be in touch. Meanwhile—you know nothing about the calculator and you talk to no-one about tonight.

Max nods

You forget Crane. You forget he ever came here. And, most important of all, you forget the people I sent for. Is that clear?

Max (*quietly*) Yes.
Digby Quite clear?
Max Quite clear.

Digby nods. He exits R

There is a disturbed look on Max's face as he moves down to the desk. He stands for a long while just staring at the photograph. Eventually he places the photograph on the desk and, crossing to the drinks table, picks up a decanter. His thoughts are still on the photograph as he prepares to pour himself a drink—then it suddenly dawns on him that the decanter he is holding is virtually empty. He puts it down and walks towards the kitchen. Max has almost reached the kitchen door when he hears a noise. He stops, and half turns towards the hall

Harriet (*off; calling*) Max . . . ?
Max There's no-one here, Harriet! Come along in . . .

Pause

Harriet enters. She is immediately relieved to find that Crane's body is no longer in the room

Harriet (*tensely*) I'm sorry, Max! I just couldn't go on sitting in that wine bar any longer!
Max (*quietly*) I said I'd phone you.
Harriet Yes, I know you did! But—what happened? Tell me! Did Dave's friend arrive?
Max Yes, he arrived.
Harriet Well?
Max (*suddenly*) Sit down, Harriet. I'm just going to get a bottle of Scotch. I'll be with you in a minute.

To Harriet's astonishment Max turns and goes into the kitchen

Harriet doesn't sit down. Instead, she nervously opens her handbag and starts searching for a packet of cigarettes. She fails to find the package and eventually crosses the room and helps herself to a cigarette from a box on the desk. She is taking a lighter out of her handbag when she notices the photograph. As Harriet picks up the photograph . . .

Max returns from the kitchen carrying a bottle of whisky

Pause

Harriet Who gave you this photograph?

Max crosses to the drinks table, puts the bottle down, then turns towards her

Max It doesn't do you justice, Harriet. (*Pause. He is gazing at her steadily*) Why didn't you tell me Terry Wilde was a friend of yours?
Harriet Terry Wilde? What are you talking about?
Max I'm talking about the man in the photograph. (*Pointing*) The man sitting next to you, outside the café.
Harriet His name's Stout! Not Wilde . . .

Max Stout?

Harriet Yes. We were staying at the same hotel in the South of France and he just wouldn't leave me alone.

Max (*quietly; watching her*) It's the man I met in Munich. Terry Wilde. The man that was murdered.

Harriet (*shaking her head*) You're mistaken! His name's Harry Stout. He's a motor-car salesman from Harrogate.

Max Is that what he told you?

Harriet Yes—and it's true. He had a car—a Porsche—with a sticker on it. "When in doubt buy from Stout".

Max When did you first meet this man?

Harriet (*reacting angrily*) What do you mean—when did I first meet him? I didn't meet him! I've told you! He was staying at the same hotel and he just wouldn't leave me alone!

Max (*his eyes still on her*) Tell me about him. Tell me everything you know about him.

Harriet There's nothing to tell, except that—he had a room next to mine and was determined to get friendly with me.

Max Was he already at the hotel when you arrived?

Harriet No, he arrived after me. I'm not sure when. I think perhaps it was the next morning.

Max Go on …

Harriet (*a shade bewildered*) What—what is it you want to know about him?

Max You say he wouldn't leave you alone?

Harriet Yes. He never stopped pestering me. I just couldn't get rid of him.

Max takes the photograph from her, stares at it, then looks at Harriet again

I know what you're thinking! The day before I left Beaulieu I went down to this café near the harbour. I'd just ordered a drink when Stout arrived. Usually the little horror was full of himself but on this occasion he was very subdued. He said he'd heard that I was leaving the next day and he wanted to apologize for having made such a nuisance of himself. He seemed genuinely sorry so I … invited him to have a drink with me …

Max Go on …

Harriet (*still puzzled*) Go on? That's it. There's nothing more I can tell you about him. He was only with me about fifteen minutes.

Max Did he know who you were?

Harriet Yes, he knew …

Max Was that the last you saw of him?

Harriet No, I bumped into him the next morning. He wanted to drive me to the airport but I wouldn't let him. (*She is looking at the photograph again*) If this is Terry Wilde …

Max It is, I assure you …

Harriet Then—why call himself Harry Stout?

Harriet sits on the sofa whilst Max appears to be giving her question thought

Max He was only with you for about a quarter of an hour?

Harriet At the café? Yes. It couldn't have been much longer.

Max What did you talk about?

Harriet So far as I recall, nothing of importance. The weather. Food. The hotel we were staying in.

Max Was I mentioned at all?

Harriet You're always mentioned, Max. He said he'd read several of your books. Now, perhaps you'll satisfy my curiosity! Who gave you this photograph?

Max (*after hesitating*) Dave's friend—Graham Digby.

Harriet Where did he get it from?

Max According to all accounts, from a colleague of his in the South of France. It was taken from a boat.

Pause

Harriet (*uneasily*) Do you believe what I've told you? Do you believe my story?

Max (*after a moment*) Yes, I believe you.

Harriet You don't sound very convinced. (*A tiny pause*) What happened after I left here? Please tell me! (*Sensing his reluctance to confide in her*) You've got to tell me, Max! I want to know what happened!

Max Digby made a phone call and ... some people came ...

Harriet Well?

Max They took Crane away. After they'd gone Digby started questioning me. He couldn't understand how I'd managed to get the better of Crane. But in the end, I think he realized I had no alternative but to defend myself.

As Max finishes speaking there is the sound of the front door closing, and Harriet rises and together with Max looks towards the hall

A somewhat agitated Liz suddenly appears

Why, hello, Liz!

Liz Max, I'm terribly sorry to disturb you!

Max That's all right. What is it?

Liz There's something I must tell you! Something I feel you ought to know ...

Max What is it, Liz?

Harriet makes a move

Liz Don't go Harriet! I'd like you to hear what I've got to say.

Harriet You're worried, Liz. What's happened?

Max Sit down, and let me get you a drink.

Liz No please! First—let me tell you why I'm here. (*A small pause, during which she collects her thoughts*) After I left you this afternoon I did some shopping and arrived home at about ten to seven. (*A slight pause*) Just as I was about to let myself into the flat, I had a strange feeling. I find it almost impossible to describe. I suppose, in a way—it was a premonition.

Max A premonition?

Max Yes.
Harriet (*sitting on the sofa*) What do you mean, Liz?

Max joins Harriet

Liz I had the feeling that there was someone in the flat . . . waiting for me . . .
Harriet Waiting for you?
Liz Yes.

Pause

Max And was there?
Liz Yes, Max, there was. An American—a man I'd never seen before—was sitting in one of the armchairs. He said his name was Lloyd Mitchell . . .
Harriet Lloyd Mitchell? That's the man that questioned Marsha!
Liz That's right.

Max, instantly curious, looks at Harriet

Max He questioned Marsha?
Harriet Yes.
Max (*sharply; concerned*) When?
Harriet Several days ago.
Max Go on, Liz!
Liz He said he very much wanted to see a copy of your diary and he'd make it well worth my while if I could get him one. I told him there were only three copies in existence and they were mostly under lock and key. Apart from which, it was more than my job was worth to let him see a copy.
Max What did he say?
Liz He simply asked me if I'd answer one or two questions. By this time, I must admit, I was curious. I told him I was not mad on games. Either on or off television. But what was it he wanted to know? (*Thoughtfully, obviously recalling the incident*) His first question puzzled me. I just couldn't see what he was getting at. (*Looking at Max; puzzled*) He wanted to know whether you'd found a calculator in your suitcase on your return from Munich.
Harriet A calculator?
Liz Yes, Harriet. (*To Max*) I said I hadn't the slightest idea what was in your case, and indeed it was none of my business! He then, much to my annoyance, started talking about the diary again. Asking all sorts of questions.
Max Questions, about what?
Liz About people. People you've mentioned in the diary.
Max Who, for instance?
Liz He particularly wanted to know if you'd written anything about Jeff Seago.
Max (*surprised*) About Jeff?
Harriet The golf professional?
Liz Yes.
Max Why was he interested in Jeff Seago?
Liz I don't know.

Max You didn't ask him?
Liz No, I'm afraid I didn't. I realize now I should have done. But at that point I lost my temper. I said under no circumstances was I prepared to discuss the contents of the diary with him—or anyone else for that matter.

Max gives a little nod of approval

Max Quite right, Liz ...
Harriet Then what happened?
Liz I asked him to leave. Well—asked ... My exact words, if I remember rightly, were "Please get to hell out of here!"
Harriet (*amused*) And did he?
Liz Yes, he did. (*She produces a card*) But not before handing me this card. (*Giving Harriet the card*) He said if I changed my mind about the diary, I could leave a message for him at that number ...

Harriet stares at the card, then hands it to Max. Max glances at the card, then puts it in his pocket

After Mitchell left I didn't know what to do. I felt ... quite shaken ... It wasn't a very pleasant experience, finding a stranger in the flat ...
Harriet I'm sure ...
Liz But don't get the wrong impression. He didn't threaten me. Not in any way ... Eventually, I poured myself a large Scotch and it was while I was drinking it that I suddenly realized that—although I had a dinner date—I must see you, Max, and tell you what had transpired ...
Max Thank you, Liz. (*He is thoughtful, slowly turning over in his mind what Liz has told him*)
Liz Who is this man Mitchell? Do you know?
Max No, I don't.
Liz Have you met him?

Max shakes his head

And why question me about a calculator?

Max makes no comment

Forgive my asking, Max, but—did you find one amongst your belongings?

Max rises and turns his back on Harriet for a moment

Max No, I didn't.

Harriet looks at Max surprised by his move. She suspects that he is lying

Liz When Harriet first told me about him I thought he was a journalist. I was convinced of it in fact. But I was wrong. He's not a newspaper man, I'm sure of that now.
Harriet Then who do you think he is?
Liz I don't know, Harriet. I'm puzzled. He's not, by any means, an unlikeable person, and yet—for the life of me I can't imagine what he's up

to. (*To Max*) Why on earth did he want to know if there was a reference to Jeff Seago in the diary? Is he a friend of Jeff's, do you think?

Max (*not wishing to be questioned*) I wouldn't know. I've certainly never heard Jeff mention him.

Liz glances at her watch and is surprised by the time

Liz Max, I'd better go. I'm having dinner with some friends and I'm terribly late already.

Max Yes, of course.

Liz I hope you don't think I've made a fuss over nothing. I do sometimes, I'm afraid.

Max You did the right thing, Liz.

As Liz moves towards the hall the phone rings and she turns and looks at Max

Liz Shall I take it?

Max Would you, Liz? I don't wish to talk to anyone at the moment.

Liz picks up the phone

Liz (*on the phone*) Hello? . . . Yes, it is. . . . I'm sorry, I can't hear you. Speak up, please. . . . (*To Max*) It's from a call-box. . . . I'm sorry, Mr Telligan's not available at the moment. Who is it speaking? . . . Miss—I'm sorry, I didn't catch your name? . . . Palmer. . . . Yes, well, I'm afraid you can't, not at the moment, Miss Palmer. I suggest you ring again, later in the week. (*She replaces the receiver*)

Max A Miss Palmer? I don't know anyone by that name? Do you, Liz?

Liz No, I don't. She sounded worried; quite agitated.

Max (*trying to recall the name*) Palmer . . .

Harriet (*softly; a shade hesitantly*) Would it be Connie Palmer?

Both Max and Liz look at Harriet, somewhat surprised

Max Who's Connie Palmer?

Harriet Isn't she the girl that Jeff Seago's friendly with?

Max I wouldn't know.

Harriet I think you'll find that's who she is.

Max (*puzzled*) How come you know this girl, Harriet?

Harriet I once gave her a lift in my car. A short, pretty little girl.

Max (*curious*) When was this?

Harriet Oh—some time ago. I forget just when. I'd dropped you at the club and I was just driving away when she asked me if I'd give her a lift.

Max Connie Palmer? (*A moment, then, suddenly*) You're right! Absolutely right! Fancy your remembering! Full Marks, Harriet! Now what the devil does she want, I wonder?

Liz Max, I must fly! I really must!

Max Yes, of course.

Liz Goodbye, Harriet.

Harriet (*her thoughts elsewhere*) Goodbye, Liz.

Liz exits

Max turns towards Harriet again

Max Is it true this man questioned Marsha?
Harriet Yes.
Max When?
Harriet Several days ago.
Max What happened?
Harriet He bought a copy of *Still Life* from her and got talking about your books. He said he was a fan of yours. When he learnt who Marsha was he asked her if she'd read any of the diary.
Max And what did Marsha say?
Harriet What could she say? (*Rising*) She told him she hadn't seen the diary, let alone read it.

Max looks at her, struck by the note of unfriendliness in her voice

Max What is it, Harriet?

Pause

Harriet Why did you lie to Liz?
Max (*taken aback*) Lie to her? What are you talking about?
Harriet You know perfectly well what I'm talking about! You've met this man Mitchell! You knew about the calculator! You were not a bit surprised when Liz mentioned it.

A tense pause

I'm right, aren't I?

Pause

Well, Max?
Max (*quietly*) Yes, I've met Mitchell. He came to the flat.
Harriet What happened? Tell me!
Max I'm sorry, Harriet, I can't. I promised Digby I wouldn't say a word about this affair to anyone.
Harriet I'm not anyone! (*Angrily*) Now look, Max! Mitchell went out of his way to question Marsha and Terry Wilde went out of his way to get friendly with me! So I want to know—I've a right to know—what this is all about?
Max I can't tell you what it's all about, for the simple reason that I don't know! And that's the truth.
Harriet But surely, you must have some idea?

A strained silence

Max, I hate to remind you of this, but if I hadn't turned up when I did God know what would have happened to you! It was me that talked you into telephoning Dave Hamley, remember.
Max I'm acutely aware of that, Harriet. And I'm more than grateful, believe me.

Harriet Then for heaven's sake trust me, and tell me all you know about this American!

Max I know nothing about him except that ... he broke into the flat and started searching for something. When I disturbed him he told me he was looking for a calculator which Terry Wilde had given me. This was the first I'd heard of a calculator but later, after he'd left, I came across one in my case.

Harriet Why did he want the calculator, do you know?

Max No, I don't. I can't imagine why he wanted it. (*After a moment, with an undertone of bewilderment in his voice*) But the thing I don't understand, the thing that puzzles me more than the calculator, is why Mitchell was curious about Jeff Seago. Why he particularly wanted to know if I'd written anything about him.

Harriet Have you? Is there a reference to him in the diary?

Max Yes, there's several references. (*Thoughtfully*) One in particular ...

Harriet Oh?

Max A rather curious thing happened, Harriet. (*After a pause*) About ten days ago I drove down to Chichester to see my agent. He's just bought a house near there. Towards the end of the journey I took the wrong turning and driving down a quiet country lane I suddenly saw Jeff. He didn't see me and since I was late for my appointment I didn't stop. (*He pauses*) I was due to play golf with him the next day and when I arrived at Midway he was waiting for me in the clubhouse.

The Lights start to fade down

During the Black-out, Harriet and Max exit, and Jeff and Connie enter with drinks and sit at the table

The Lights come up on the table in the alcove. Jeff Seago and Connie Palmer are sitting at the table. They have drinks in front of them. Connie is in her twenties

Jeff It's too expensive. No dress is worth that sort of money.

Connie Well—think about it.

Jeff It's just not on, Connie. In more ways than one.

Connie (*good-natured*) Ho-ho! Very funny! You're just a mean bastard, that's your trouble. Here's your friend ...

Max arrives at the table

Jeff (*rising*) Hello, Max ...

Max Sorry I'm late. The traffic was appalling. It won't take me long to change.

Jeff You're not late, squire, and there's no hurry. (*He sits*) There's a geriatric four ball on the first tee, so there's bound to be a bit of a hold up. Sit down and have a drink ...

Rose, a club stewardess, appears

Rose Can I get you anything, sir?

Max Er—no thank you, Rose.

Jeff Are you sure?
Max Yes. (*He sits*) I won't have a drink, if you don't mind.

Rose goes

Jeff Frightened you won't be able to keep your eye on the ball, is that it!
Max It's not just that. It could very easily ruin my slice.

Jeff laughs

Jeff (*suddenly*) Oh, I'm sorry? I don't think you know Connie.
Connie Hi!
Max How are you, my dear?
Connie I'm in a very bad mood. He's just refused to buy me an absolutely smashing dress.
Max Yes, I know. I heard him.
Jeff (*grinning*) It wouldn't do anything for her, squire. Too cheap. Only three hundred quid.
Connie They said they'd reduce it.
Jeff Big deal.

A tiny pause

Max I was surprised to see you yesterday afternoon, Jeff. What were you doing in that part of the world?

Jeff looks at him

Jeff What part of the world, Max?
Max I went down to Chichester to see a friend of mine. I got lost and driving down a country lane I suddenly saw you, Jeff. I was very surprised I must say.
Jeff (*staring at him oddly*) You saw me, in a country lane, yesterday afternoon?
Max Well, actually, you'd just come out of a cottage and you were standing near a beehive talking to a tall, dark-looking man.
Jeff (*amused*) Was this before or after lunch, squire?
Max (*puzzled*) I saw you, Jeff. Quite clearly. The cottage was called "High Trees".
Jeff "High Trees"? (*Shaking his head*) I can assure you, it wasn't me you saw, Max. (*He looks at Connie*) I wouldn't get within a hundred miles of a beehive, would I, honey? (*With a grin, suddenly realizing what he has said*) Oh! Sorry about that . . .
Connie Where was this cottage?
Max Somewhere between Midhurst and Chichester.
Jeff Never been in that neck of the woods, old man—not so far as I can recall. As a matter of fact, I took the day off yesterday and the pair of us went up to Town. (*To Connie*) That's right, isn't it?

She nods

We had lunch, dropped into Selfridges for an hour or so, and finished up seeing a movie.

Max hesitates, then gives a non-commital shake of the head

Max I could have sworn it was you, Jeff. Well—there's only one explana-
tion. You've got a double, or a look-alike, as they say these days.
Jeff Poor devil . . .
Connie Let's hope he's not a mean little sod like you, darling.

Jeff laughs and makes a face at her

   Rose appears

Rose (*to Jeff*) Excuse me, sir. You're wanted on the phone.
Jeff Who is it?
Rose Need you ask, Mr Seago? It's the Secretary.
Jeff Oh—thank you, Rose.

   Rose goes

   (*Rising from the table*) Well—it makes a nice change. I'm usually in the
   bath or on the loo when the old boy insists on talking to me. Excuse me.

   He goes

*Pause. Max appears lost in thought, then he suddenly realizes that Connie is
looking at him*

Max I'm sorry. Would you care for another drink?
Connie I'd better not. I've had two already. (*After a pause*) You write
books, or something, don't you?
Max Books.
Connie Did you write *The Day of the Jackass*?
Max Jackal.
Connie Jackal?
Max *The Day of the Jackal*. No, unfortunately I didn't. Have you read it?
Connie No, but I saw the movie. It was super.
Max Yes, it was. Was that the film you saw yesterday?
Connie No, no, it was on the box. It's an oldie.
Max Yes, I suppose it must be, by now. (*After a pause*) Do you often go to
the cinema?
Connie No, not often. Jeff has a video. We watch that most of the time.
Max (*apparently making conversation*) Who's your favourite actor these
days?
Connie Oh, I don't know. I keep changing my mind.
Max Who was in the film you saw yesterday?
Connie (*uneasily*) Yesterday? Oh—it was a French fella. Don't ask me his
name.
Max If it was a French film I've probably seen it. I see most of them. What
was it called?
Connie Oh, dear! I thought you were going to ask me that! I'm terrible on
titles. And if I did remember it, I wouldn't be able to pronounce it.
Max Well—which cinema was it?

Pause

The Curzon?

As Connie still hesitates

That's the one in Curzon Street.
Connie (*laughing*) Yes, it would be, wouldn't it! Look—I'm sorry, I really
can't remember. To be honest, I was bored stiff. I slept through most of
the film.
Max That can happen. Especially if you've had a good lunch. (*He smiles at
her. A tiny pause*) A friend of mine slept through *Gone With The Wind*.
And it was the first time he'd seen it. Except that he didn't see it, of course.

A slightly uncomfortable pause, then Max rises

Well—I'd better get ready for the thrashing I'm about to receive at the
hands of your boy friend.
Connie Have a nice game.
Max Thank you.

Max goes

Connie obviously relieved at his departure, continues sitting at the table

The Lights go down

During the Black-out, Connie exits, taking the glasses with her

The Lights gradually rise to reveal Max with Harriet

Harriet You think Jeff was lying?
Max I think they both were, Harriet.
Harriet People do have look-alikes, you know. I remember a hairdresser I
used to go to. She was accused of stealing a handbag and it was
discovered she had a look-alike.
Max It was Jeff Seago I saw that afternoon! No-one else! I'm convinced of
it!
Harriet Well—I daresay there's a perfectly simple explanation. Perhaps Jeff
doesn't want anyone at Midway Park to know about the cottage?
Max Why not?
Harriet Maybe he's been making money on the side, without the club
knowing, and the cottage belongs to him.
Max That's a possibility, I suppose.

Pause. Harriet is studying him

Harriet But you're not convinced?
Max No, somehow, I'm not, and I don't quite know why. It's just that—I
have a gut feeling there's more to it than that.

Pause

Harriet You say, he was standing outside a cottage, talking to someone?
Max Yes. A tall, swarthy looking chap in jeans and a sports jacket. I had
the impression I'd seen him before somewhere, but I couldn't place him.

Then later, when I was writing the diary, I seemed to remember that I'd seen a picture of him in one of the Sunday newspapers.

Harriet In one of the papers?

Max Yes, but I couldn't remember what they'd written about him.

Pause

Harriet How well do you know Jeff?

Max We've played quite a bit of golf together during the past year or so and I've had several lessons from him. But he's not a close friend, not by any means.

Harriet Would you trust him?

Max Trust him? (*A moment*) With my car, yes. But not my daughter.

Harriet smiles and moves towards the hall

Well, that's about it. There's nothing else I can tell you about him. Except that ... I'm sure—absolutely sure—it was Jeff I saw that afternoon.

Harriet (*with a little nod*) I think it must have been. Max, I must go! I've got to get up early tomorrow morning. Marsha's having the morning off and there's a sale we both want to go to.

Max When are you returning to the house?

Harriet I haven't decided.

Max I'll phone you.

Harriet Yes, do that.

They look at each other for a brief moment, then exit into the hall together

After a pause, Max returns and, crossing to the desk, looks at the photograph again. He is about to put it in one of the drawers, then changing his mind, he replaces it on the desk and picks up the phone. He dials

Max (*on the phone*) Marsha? ... Yes, it is ... I've just been talking to your mother, Marsha. ... Yes, she's staying the night in Town. ... Tell me, my dear—when your mother got back from the South of France did she say anything to you about a man called Stout? ... Yes, Stout. ... A car salesman from Harrogate. ... He was staying at the same hotel. ...

The doorbell rings

No, no, it was just that she mentioned him and I wondered whether she'd spoken to you about him? ...

The doorbell is heard again. Max turns his head and looks towards the hall

Marsha, I'm sorry, there's someone at the door. I'll ring you back later, my dear ...

Max puts the receiver down and goes out into the hall

Pause. We hear voices: then Connie Palmer enters with Max

Connie (*agitatedly apologetic*) I promise you I won't keep you long. I tried to talk to you on the phone. I rang you from the box on the corner, but the woman who spoke to me said——

Max (*weighing her up; yet quite friendly*) It was my secretary. I'm sorry I couldn't speak to you. I had someone with me at the time. Let me take your coat ...

Connie No, no, I can't stay ...

Max Well—please sit down.

Connie hesitates, then crosses to one of the armchairs. Pause

What is it you want to see me about? (*After a pause*) Is it something to do with Jeff? (*He sits on the sofa, facing her*)

Connie Yes, it is. We've had a flaming row and ... Do you know a woman called Clare Bellinger?

Max I've met her. She's a member of Midway Park.

Connie Yes. Jeff's been giving her lessons. (*Vehemently*) In more ways than one, the little shit!

Max He's having an affair with her, is that it?

Connie Not only that, he's moved in with her and taken everything with him. Every bloody thing. Even the bloody video.

Max I'm sorry ...

Connie Yes, well—he's not going to get away with it!

Max Forgive me, but from what you've just told me, it rather sounds as if he has got away with it.

Connie I had three thousand pounds of my own when I met Jeff. Three thousand quid! And it's gone! Every penny! One way and another he's had the lot. (*She pauses*) Anyway, that's not your worry. That's not why I came here.

Max (*quietly; watching her*) Why did you come here, Connie?

Connie I came here because I think it's only fair that you should know ... Look—I'm sorry! I lied to you the other week. Jeff and I didn't go to a movie. We didn't spend the day together in London, like he said. He left the house in the morning, as usual, and we didn't see each other again until the evening.

Max I see.

Connie He's thinking of leaving Midway Park and he'd heard of a vacancy at a club near Chichester. He went down there to take a look at the course. Afterwards he had lunch with a friend of his. The man who owns the cottage.

Max Is that what he told you?

Connie Yes. He recognized your car when you drove past the cottage and he was worried. He said under no circumstances must you, or anyone else, suspect that he wanted to leave Midway. He said if the club got wind of it, he'd get the chop.

Max And you believed his story?

Connie I sort of—half believed it ...

Max Tell me about this friend of Jeff's. The man he had lunch with.

Connie I know nothing at all about him. I asked him who he was but he simply said he was a mate and that they were at Cambridge together.

Max Did he tell you his name?

Connie No.

Max Had he ever mentioned him before?

Connie shakes her head

Or the cottage?

Connie No, never. (*A small pause*) But there is something, something I don't understand . . .

Max Go on, Connie.

Connie Just recently Jeff's been getting an awful lot of phone calls, usually late at night, sometimes when we're in bed. And they've got nothing to do with golf or Midway Park, I'm sure of that.

Max What makes you so sure?

Connie Well, for one thing the caller's usually a foreigner . . .

Max Foreigners play golf.

Connie Yes, but invariably Jeff asks them to ring back so he can take the call in his study, without my overhearing what's being said.

Max Have you ever picked up the receiver and listened to one of these calls?

Connie No, I haven't. But I must admit I've been tempted.

Max (*after a thoughtful pause; rising*) Well—thank you for coming, my dear, and telling me all this. I appreciate it.

Connie (*getting up*) I hope the club find out about Jeff and he gets the chopper! The son of a bitch deserves it, after the way he's treated me.

They move towards the hall

Max What are you going to do now?

Connie I suppose I shall have to start work again. Whether I'll be able to get my old job back, I just don't know. It's doubtful.

Max What was your last job?

Connie Oh, dear! Don't laugh.

Max Why should I laugh?

Connie I was a traffic warden.

Max I'll keep a sharp look-out for you, Connie. Good luck, my dear.

Connie exits

Max turns and goes into the bedroom

Pause. Suddenly there is the sound of a disturbance in the hall, followed by a terrified scream and the slamming of the front door

Max rushes out of the bedroom

Connie staggers into the room from the hall. She has been brutally attacked. Her face slashed. There is blood on her hands and dress

My God! What happened? (*He quickly puts his arms around her and helps her towards the sofa*) I'll get a doctor!

As Connie sinks on to the sofa, distressed and in obvious pain, Max is at the desk desperately dialling for help

Black-out

The same. The following morning

Max is sitting in an armchair watching Jeff Seago who is agitatedly pacing up and down the room. Jeff finally comes to rest at the drinks table and stubs out the cigarette he has been smoking

Jeff Max, forgive me, but—I don't think you have the slightest idea how desperately worried I've been! Even now, I find myself . . . (*He shakes his head in despair*) That this should have happened to Connie, of all people!

Max She's going to be all right, Jeff. I've spoken to the hospital.

Jeff Yes, but—what happened? What exactly happened? I'm still in the dark!

Max (*rising*) Didn't the police tell you what happened?

Jeff They simply said she'd paid you a visit and on leaving here she was attacked by someone.

Max nods

They questioned me for the best part of an hour.

Max That was to be expected, I'm afraid.

Jeff (*moving down to Max*) What d'you mean, that was to be expected?

Max My dear fellow, you've been living with the girl for almost two years and you recently had a row with her! It was obvious that the police would want to question you!

Jeff (*after a moment*) Who told you about the row? Connie?

Max Yes.

Jeff (*quietly*) What else did she tell you?

Max She said you'd walked out on her.

Jeff Go on! What else?

Max She said you were having an affair with Clare Bellinger.

Jeff Clare Bellinger?

Max Yes.

Jeff (*derisively*) You've got to be joking!

Max That's what she said.

Jeff I wouldn't shack up with that nymphomaniac if you paid me! Look— let's get the record straight! I did have a row with Connie and I did walk out on her. But it's not the first time. We've been having rows for weeks, for months now. Believe me, Max, she's just impossible to live with these days. But you still haven't answered my question. What actually happened here last night?

Max Someone—the assailant—was waiting for Connie, either in the hall or outside the front door. We're not sure which.

Jeff Did she recognize the bastard?

Max I think she must have done, but she refuses to say who it was, or even discuss the incident.

Jeff She's scared. Scared to death, poor darling. And it's not surprising. Thank God I was able to convince the police I wasn't anywhere near here when it happened. At least—I think I convinced them . . .

Max Then you've nothing to worry about.

Jeff I've a great deal to worry about! I'm still fond of Connie. I want to know who attacked her. And why?

Max So do I. And I was hoping you might be able to throw some light on that, Jeff.

Jeff (*shaking his head*) I'm completely bewildered. I just can't imagine why anyone would do such a terrible thing.

Pause

Max Have you seen Connie?

Jeff No, I haven't. The hospital said she didn't wish to see anyone. Not even her mother.

Another pause. Jeff is looking at Max, quietly sizing him up. Max is suddenly aware of this

I didn't know Connie was a friend of yours, Max.

Max She's not a friend of mine. I hardly know her.

Jeff Then why did she come here?

Max She came because—she thought it was about time I was told the truth.

Jeff The truth? About what? (*A sudden realization*) Oh! About the cottage! About your seeing me that day, near Chichester?

Max nods

Well, there's a perfectly simple explanation. For some time now I've been thinking of leaving Midway and I recently heard of a job going in Sussex. I went down there to take a look at the course. On the way home I dropped in on an old friend of mine.

Max Why didn't you tell me that at the time? Why make up that story about spending the day in London?

Jeff I just didn't want you, or anyone else at the club, to know what I was up to.

Max Why not?

Jeff Come on, Max! Use your imagination! You know the Midway crowd. If they thought I was thinking of leaving they'd immediately get rid of me on some pretext or other.

Max I still don't understand why you didn't confide in me?

Jeff I should have done, of course. I realize that now. But I was afraid you might inadvertently say something to one of the members. Anyway, that's all there is to it. (*He moves towards the hall, then suddenly hesitates*)

Max What is it, Jeff?

Jeff Did Connie really tell you I was having an affair with Clare Bellinger?

Max Of course she did! Do you think I made it up?

Jeff Clare Bellinger! Ye gods, I'd be dead in a week. They don't call her intensive Clare for nothing.

They exit into the hall

After a pause, Max returns and crossing the room opens the door down R

Graham Digby enters; he carries his briefcase

Max I'm sorry we were interrupted, but he insisted on seeing me.

Digby nods and moves down to one of the armchairs

Would you care for some coffee before we continue our talk?

Digby Later, perhaps. (*Sitting in the chair*) You were about to tell me what the hospital said?

Max They said Miss Palmer was comfortable and they expected her to be discharged at the end of the week. I was relieved to hear it.

Pause

Digby She left the hospital this morning, Mr Telligan.

Max (*staring at him; astonished*) This morning?

Digby Yes. About an hour after you telephoned.

Max (*puzzled*) Why this morning?

Digby We thought it advisable. (*After a pause*) We have a house in Berkshire. It's in lovely surroundings, well staffed, the food's excellent, and there's a resident doctor. Miss Palmer will be very well looked after, I assure you. There's only one problem.

Max What's that?

Digby When the time comes she won't wish to leave. They never do.

Max They?

Digby People we have to protect from time to time.

Max crosses down to Digby and stands quietly looking down at him

Max You know, I've read about you. People like you, I mean. But to be perfectly honest, I've never really thought you existed. I've always thought you were just a figment of the imagination.

Digby (*drily*) I have a feeling you're pulling my leg, Mr Telligan.

Max Yes, I'm pulling your leg. (*After a small pause; deadly serious*) Who are you, Digby?

Silence

Who do you work for?

Silence

MI five?

Silence

MI six?

Silence?

MI seven? MI eight? MI nine? SIS? SAS? Who the devil are you?

Digby Let's just say, I'm the man who saved you from facing a murder charge—and leave it at that. (*With quiet authority*) Now, please sit down. I've got something to tell you.

Max About Miss Palmer?

Digby No, not about Miss Palmer.

Max, obviously curious, moves to one of the chairs

Mr Telligan, why do you think Terry Wilde was murdered?

Max (*sitting*) I don't know why. I haven't the faintest idea.

Digby Wilde was a CIA agent.

Max (*stunned*) Terry Wilde? Are you serious?

Digby I'm quite serious. He was investigating a terrorist organization which has been responsible for the deaths of several Americans and, indeed, many of our own people. We're interested in this organization because three of their most important members have actually been based here, in the UK. A fortnight ago—on April eighteenth to be precise—another member of the group, a man known simply as Emile, arrived here from Paris. We were waiting for him, but with the help of his colleagues, he slipped through our fingers and went into hiding.

Max But who are his colleagues? Who are these people?

Digby Wilde discovered the identity of one of them and was in the process of passing this information on to another CIA man—Lloyd Mitchell— when he was shot. The calculator you brought back contained a microfilm showing a meeting between Emile and the man in question. Crane. (*After a pause*) We think we know who the other two are, but we're not certain. We've had several people under surveillance during the past few weeks.

Max Including my wife, no doubt?

Digby Yes, including your wife. And I know exactly what you're about to say! "Does my wife look like a terrorist?" No, of course she doesn't! But the important people, the people behind the scenes, never do . . .

Max But are you suggesting that my wife——

Digby (*affably*) I'm not suggesting anything! It was you that mentioned your wife, Mr Telligan. Nevertheless, you'd be wise to bear in mind what I've just told you. The people who count—who really count—never do look like terrorists. As a matter of fact, they're so God-damned ordinary, it just isn't true! Which is a problem we're constantly coming up against. (*Opening his case and taking out the diary*) I read your diary last night. In fact it was two o'clock in the morning when I put it down.

Max I'm glad it held your interest.

Digby It did more than that. A great deal more. Firstly, it justified the interest we—and certain other people—have taken in the diary. Secondly, it convinced me more than ever, that you haven't the slightest idea just how important some of your observations are.

Max Important to whom?

Digby To us, Mr Telligan.

Max What observations! What are you referring to?

Digby opens the diary to a page he has already marked

Digby Well, take for example, the entry you made on April eighteenth.

Max April eighteenth?

Digby Yes.

Max (*staring at him; oddly*) But that's the date you mentioned.

Digby That's right.

Max (*puzzled*) What did I write on April eighteenth? I can't remember.

Digby You can't?

Max (*thoughtfully*) No, I'm afraid I can't. Please tell me.

Digby I've every intention of telling you, Mr Telligan, because we're going to need your help. And in the very near future, unless I'm mistaken. (*Suddenly, smiling*) But first, do you think I might change my mind about the coffee?

Max Why, yes. Yes, of course.

Max stares at Digby, curious—then he turns and goes into the kitchen

There is a watchful pause, before Digby replaces the diary in his case, rises, and crosses to the telephone. He stands for a second or two looking towards the kitchen, then he takes a magnetic object—a "bugging" device—out of his pocket and starts to dismantle the receiver. He is attaching the device to the phone when . . .

The Lights fade

SCENE 3

The same. Late Wednesday afternoon

Liz enters from the hall carrying a bunch of flowers wrapped in cellophane. She crosses to the desk, puts the flowers down, and is taking off her things, when . . .

Max comes out of the bedroom carrying his hat and coat

Liz stares at him, obviously surprised to find him in the flat

Liz Why, hello, Max! Have you forgotten your appointment? You're supposed to be seeing your accountants at five o'clock.

Max Yes, I know. I haven't forgotten. I'm running late. What are the flowers in aid of?

Liz They're for our trendy friend upstairs. There was no reply and the poor little man from the florists didn't know what to do with them.

Max Good heavens, isn't that girl ever in? We shall have to start charging her, Liz!

Liz I've dropped a note through her letter box, she'll pick them up later.

Max If you take my advice you'll deliver them. If she comes down here she'll talk your head off and you'll never get rid of her.

Liz I imagine you've heard about Jeff Seago?

Max looks at her

His girl friend—Connie Palmer, I think her name is—was mugged last night. I heard Jeff Seago talking about it on the radio.

Max (*surprised*) He was on the radio?

Liz Yes, he was interviewed by someone.

A slight pause

Max It happened here, Liz. Shortly after you left.

Liz (*astonished*) It happened here? (*Bewildered*) You mean—here, in the flat?

Max Yes. She was just letting herself out of the flat when she was attacked by someone.

Liz How awful! Is she going to be all right?

Max I think so. But the poor girl's had to have an awful lot of stitches in her face.

Liz (*puzzled*) You say, this happened soon after I left?

Max Yes.

Liz Was Harriet still here?

Max No, she'd just gone. I was in the bedroom and I suddenly heard someone screaming.

Liz Have the police any idea who did it?

Max If they have, they haven't confided in me.

A pause. Liz is hesitating

Liz Is Miss Palmer a friend of yours? Forgive my asking, Max, but——

Max No, she's not a friend of mine. (*Turning towards the hall*) I hardly know her. She came to see me because . . . Look, I'll put you in the picture later, Liz. Will you be here when I get back?

Liz It's possible. I've several letters to type and I've still got the Australian contract to finish.

Max nods and exits

Liz moves to the desk, sorts through various papers and eventually finds the document she is looking for. She sits at the desk quietly studying the contract. After a little while she makes an alteration to one of the clauses in the contract then places a sheet of paper in the typewriter. She is about to start typing when the doorbell rings

Liz rises and goes out into the hall

We hear the opening of the front door and the sound of voices

(*Off; annoyed*) No, I'm very sorry, you can't! I'm sorry, but it's not convenient at the moment. (*Angrily*) Didn't you hear what I said!

Lloyd Mitchell enters, quickly followed by Liz

Lloyd (*intensely annoyed*) What is this? I thought you didn't like playing games?

Liz (*taken aback*) Games? What are you talking about?

Lloyd You know perfectly well what I'm talking about! You telephoned that number I gave you and left a message saying you wished to see me . . .

Liz (*astonished*) I did?

Lloyd Yes!

Liz When?

Lloyd (*aggressively*) You know when! You don't need me to tell you!

Pause. Liz glares at him

Liz When did I telephone you? Tell me!
Lloyd It was just after eleven.
Liz This morning?
Lloyd Yes, this morning! You left a message asking me to call here.
Liz (*after a moment*) I'm sorry, I don't believe you.
Lloyd You don't believe me?
Liz No, I don't. This is a ploy! You just want to ask me a lot more questions!

Lloyd grabs hold of her arm

Lloyd Are you telling me that you didn't make that phone call?
Liz Please leave go of my arm! (*After a pause*) You heard what I said, leave go of my arm!

A tense pause. He releases her

I had a dentist's appointment at half-past ten; I was with him until a quarter-past twelve.
Lloyd Don't dentists have telephones in this God-forsaken town?
Liz They do, but I didn't make that phone call! I don't even remember your number. Now will you please leave!

A moment of uneasy silence

Lloyd Did I hurt you, just now?

A tiny pause, then Liz shakes her head

I'm sorry. I apologize. I really am sorry ...
Liz (*curious*) You say someone telephoned and left a message, asking you to call here?
Lloyd Yes. It was on my answering machine. A woman's voice said, "This is Miss Ferber. I'd like to take you up on that offer you made. Please come to Mr Telligan's apartment this evening, between five and six ..."
Liz Well, I certainly didn't leave that message, I assure you.
Lloyd It sounded like you. It sounded remarkably like you.
Liz It may have done. But it wasn't me!

An uncomfortable moment

Lloyd (*quietly*) OK! I believe you. (*His eyes on her*) And I hope you believe me, Miss Ferber.
Liz My instinct tells me not to. But—curiously enough, I do. (*She stares at him for a moment, then, not unfriendly*) Mr Mitchell, the last time we met you asked me several questions.

Lloyd nods

Now, if you don't mind, I think it's my turn to do the questioning.
Lloyd Sure. Why not? I guess that's fair enough under the circumstances. Fire ahead ...
Liz Who are you? Who do you work for? And why are you interested in Mr Telligan?

Lloyd I'm the junior partner in a Washington firm called Walker and Mitchell. I doubt whether you've heard of us.

Liz You're quite right. I haven't.

Lloyd Strictly speaking we're a law firm, but in reality—we're just a couple of high-class snoopers.

Liz And what does that mean, exactly?

Lloyd It means: should you require information about someone. A friend, an enemy, a relative maybe. Then we'd get it for you. At a price.

Liz You dig up the dirt? Is that it?

Lloyd It's not a description we care for. But, that's just about it, I guess.

Pause

Why are you looking at me like that?

Liz You're not a very good liar, are you Mr Mitchell?

Lloyd No?

Liz No. You don't look like a snooper. High-class or otherwise.

Lloyd Well, that's sure nice to know. What do I look like?

Pause

Liz You could, I suppose, be some sort of a private eye ...

Lloyd A private eye?

Liz Yes. But somehow—(*shaking her head*)—I don't think you are. If I had to put money on it, I'd say you were CIA.

Lloyd (*laughing*) You've been reading too many thrillers, Miss Ferber. (*Suddenly, serious*) Supposing I level with you. Supposing I tell you who I am and what I am——

The telephone rings

If I did that would you be prepared to ... (*He turns and looks towards the telephone*)

Liz (*crossing to the desk*) Excuse me ... (*She picks up the phone*) Hello? ... Oh, hello, Samantha. ... Yes, they're here. ... (*She looks at the flowers*) Yes, I have. ... No, don't do that, Samantha! I'll bring them up straightaway. (*She quickly puts the receiver down and turns to Lloyd*) Will you excuse me? I've got to take these flowers upstairs. I'll only be a few minutes.

Lloyd Yes, of course.

Liz picks up the flowers and exits

Pause. Lloyd surveys the room, then taking a packet of cigarettes out of his pocket he walks slowly down to the sofa. He sits on the arm of the sofa and is about to open the packet when a thought occurs to him. He returns the cigarettes to his pocket, crosses to the phone, and dials a number. Whilst the number is ringing out Lloyd picks up a stiletto-type paper-knife which is on the desk, casually turning it over in his hands

(*On the phone*) Listen carefully! There's a message on the answering machine. I want you to play it back. ... This morning, about eleven o'clock. ... (*Impatiently*) No, I don't want the message, I know what it is!

I just want to hear the voice! (*A long pause—during which he eventually hears the recorded message*) ... Yes, I heard it. Thank you. (*He replaces the receiver and sits on the desk, staring ahead away from the kitchen door, puzzled, his thoughts on the voice he has heard*)

Pause

Jeff Seago suddenly appears from the entrance to the kitchen R. *He carries a short nylon rope. He moves silently towards Lloyd*

Pause. Lloyd instinctively senses that there is someone else in the room. The moment he half turns Jeff springs forward and, whipping the rope around Lloyd's throat, pulls him away from the desk. As Jeff attempts to tighten the rope Lloyd realizes that he must make use of the knife he is holding. The moment Jeff sees the knife he releases his hold on the rope and the two men become locked in a vicious struggle. The struggle continues for some time before Jeff finally manages to overpower the American. As Jeff grasps hold of the knife Lloyd realizes that he is losing the battle and he makes a desperate attempt to free himself. Jeff immediately takes advantage of the movement, quickly plunging the knife into Llody's body. As the American falls to the ground ...

Black-out

SCENE 4

The same. Thursday morning

Max is sitting at the desk reading a newspaper. There are several other papers on the desk which have obviously been read. After a little while he puts the newspaper down and crosses to the drinks table. He has just finished getting himself a drink when ...

Liz enters

Max (*turning*) Hello, Liz ...

Liz Max ... (*She looks tense and worried as she crosses to the desk*)

Max I didn't expect to see you this morning.

Liz I've been so worried! I just had to talk to you, Max. (*She puts down the valise she is carrying*) I—I didn't sleep a wink last night ...

Max That doesn't surprise me! I should hate to tell you what sort of night I had! (*Holding up his glass*) I'm having a drink. What about you?

Liz shakes her head

Come on! You look to me as if you could use one!

Liz No, thank you, Max.

Max moves down to her

Max You've seen the papers, I imagine?

Liz Yes, I've seen them. (*A moment*) I'm terribly worried, Max. I really am! I don't think that man who questioned me, the Inspector ...

Max Superintendent.

Liz Superintendent. (*Putting her handbag on the desk*) I don't think he believed my story.

Max What makes you say that?

Liz He kept asking me the same questions over and over again. How well did I know Mitchell? Why did I take the flowers upstairs? How long was I out of the room?

Max It's his job to ask questions. After you left I had the same treatment.

Liz (*a shade relieved*) Oh. I didn't realize that. (*A small pause*) Will he want to question us again, do you think?

Max I doubt it.

Liz In a way, I hope he does. I was in such a state last night.

Max What happened when you went upstairs with the flowers? You told the Superintendent you were away about five or six minutes. Was it as long as that?

Liz Yes—it might even have been longer. Samantha didn't know who'd sent the flowers so I had a lurid description of every boy friend from the year dot. I just couldn't get away from the wretched girl. Finally, when I did manage to escape ... (*She hesitates*) ...

Max Go on, Liz ...

Liz I found Mitchell. He was dead. He—he was over there, in a pool of blood. I panicked, Max! I'm afraid there's no other word for it! I just panicked! By the time I phoned the police, I was very nearly hysterical.

There is a sympathetic pause

Max I understand Mitchell was under the impression you'd asked him to call here. Is that right?

Liz Yes. He said there was a message to that effect on his answering machine.

Max Well, obviously he was lying.

Liz No, curiously enough, I don't think he was. I think he did receive a message. I think some woman must have telephoned and said she was me. (*Her voice breaking slightly*) That's why I'm worried, Max. Desperately worried. I saw the look on the Superintendent's face when I tried to explain the situation to him.

Max stands for a moment, staring at her, then:

Max Look, to put your mind at rest I'm going to tell you something. Something I shouldn't tell you. But, under the circumstances, I think I'm more than justified. (*He pauses*) The police know who killed Mitchell.

Liz (*incredulously*) They know who killed him?

Max Yes. They arrested a man in the early hours of this morning.

Liz Who told you this?

Max Someone telephoned me.

Liz The Superintendent?

Max No, not the Superintendent.

Liz Then how do you know it's true?

Max It is true, I assure you. (*A small pause, almost a hesitation*) Lloyd

Mitchell was with the CIA and he was investigating a terrorist organiza-
tion. Jeff Seago's a member of that organization and early this——
Liz Jeff Seago!
Max Yes.

Liz is staring at him, thunderstruck

Early this morning Seago, and a man they call Emile, were picked up by
the police. Seago's been charged with the murder of Lloyd Mitchell.
Liz I don't believe this!
Max It's true, Liz.
Liz But I've known Jeff for some time! Never in my wildest——(*Suddenly, a
shade annoyed*) Who told you this? And how long have you known about
Mitchell and the CIA?
Max I'm sorry, I can't answer those questions! I've already said a great deal
more than I should have done.

Pause

Liz I—I just can't believe what you've told me! (*She shakes her head*) Are
you sure? (*Momentarily lost for words*) Absolutely . . . sure about this?
Max Yes, I'm absolutely sure.

There is a brief silence, then Max turns towards the bedroom

Liz (*stopping him*) Is there anything I can do this morning, Max? I really
must try and take my mind off what happened.

Max indicates the dictating machine on the desk

Max I did a little dictation yesterday, before I left for the accountants. And
there are several letters on the desk which need answering.

The telephone rings

(*A moment*) Would you answer it, Liz?
Liz (*picking up the phone*) Hello? . . . Yes, it is. . . . Oh, hello Marsha! . . .
What's that? . . . Yes, he is. . . . Hold on! (*To Max*) It's your daughter . . .
Max I'll take it in the bedroom.

Max, drink in hand, goes into the bedroom

Liz (*on the phone*) He's coming, Marsha . . .

*A long pause—then hearing Max's voice she replaces the receiver and turns to
the desk. Liz stands for a while, thoughtful and puzzled. Then she picks up
several letters, reading one of them, glancing at the others, finally putting them
down and switching on the machine. Pause. As she picks up her notebook and
pen, ready for the dictation, voices are heard on the tape. Liz freezes, staring at
the machine in astonishment*

On tape: the voices of Liz and Lloyd Mitchell

Lloyd's voice Why are you looking at me like that?
Liz's voice You're not a very good liar, are you, Mr Mitchell?
Lloyd's voice No?

Liz's voice No. You don't look like a snooper. High-class or otherwise.
Lloyd's voice Well, that's sure nice to know. What do I look like?
Liz's voice You could, I suppose, be some sort of a private eye . . .
Lloyd's voice A private eye?
Liz's voice Yes. But somehow—I don't think you are. If I had to put money on it, I'd say you were CIA.
Lloyd's voice You've been reading too many thrillers, Miss Ferber. Supposing I level with you. Supposing I tell you who I am and what I am—

Sound of the phone ringing

If I did that would you be prepared to . . .
Liz's voice Excuse me . . .

The sound of the phone being answered

Hello?
Jeff's voice It's Jeff! I'm in the box on the corner.
Liz's voice Oh, hello, Samantha . . .
Jeff's voice Has he arrived?
Liz's voice Yes, they're here.
Jeff's voice Have you unlocked the door?
Liz's voice Yes, I have.
Jeff's voice OK. Make yourself scarce! I'll deal with the bastard!

The sound of Jeff ringing off

Liz's voice No, don't do that Samantha! I'll bring them up straightaway.

The sound of the receiver being replaced

Will you excuse me? I've got to take these flowers upstairs. I'll only be a few minutes.
Lloyd's voice Yes, of course.

Liz's astonishment has turned to anger. She stops the machine, and picks up her handbag. She hesitates for a moment then, making a decision, she takes a gun out of the bag. Liz waits for Max to return, her eyes on the bedroom door. There is a long, tense pause

Max enters. Seeing the gun he immediately freezes

Liz (*intensely angry*) Who taped that phone call?

Silence

How did you find out about Jeff?

Silence

Tell me!

Max moves down to her and as he does to he casually picks up a cushion off the sofa

Max Before I tell you anything, put that gun down.

Liz (*shaking her head*) Not until you've told me what I want to know! And don't think I'm bluffing, Max. It won't be the first time I've used this!

Max moves a shade closer to her

Max A short time ago a man came to see me. He was a friend of Dave Hamley's. He told me that both you and Jeff Seago were members of a terrorist organization. At first, I didn't believe him, but later when I heard that Lloyd Mitchell had paid you a visit I began to suspect that you—— (*Suddenly, looking towards the hall, and exclaiming in amazement*) HAR-RIET!!!

Liz instinctively turns and Max takes full advantage of the movement, tossing the cushion at her and springing forward

As the gun falls out of her hand Liz rushes out into the hall

Max makes no attempt to follow her, instead he gives a little sigh of relief, picks up the gun, and takes it down to the desk. He is turning away from the desk when . . .

Digby enters from the kitchen, carrying his usual briefcase

(*A shade angrily*) She had a gun. (*He points to it*) Did you know that?
Digby It's a risk we have to take, from time to time.
Max *You* have to take!

Digby smiles, moves down to the desk and opens his case

Digby I'm returning your diary. I'm sure it'll be a great success, Mr Telligan, when it's published. (*He takes the diary out of the case*) Apart from our interest in Jeff Seago we were anxious to read what you'd written about your secretary. Particularly with regard to her movements. Last year for instance, according to the diary, she spent a total of sixty days outside of the UK . . .
Max Sixty days?
Digby Yes, and believe me, it wasn't just a coincidence that a number of terrorist attacks were planned during those sixty days. On April eighteenth of this year—the date I mentioned—it was announced in the press that Emile, one of the most wanted terrorists in Europe, had been arrested at London Airport. This is what you wrote in your diary on that day. (*He opens the diary at a page with a marker, and reads*) ". . . Just don't know what on earth has got into Liz today. Her thoughts appear to be miles away. One gets the impression that she is worried and anxiously awaiting news of some kind . . ."
Max Yes, I remember writing that!
Digby Unfortunately, it wasn't true about Emile. Our people made a monumental mistake. They arrested the wrong man—a decoy. Later that night the true story broke. Emile had given us the slip and had gone into hiding. This is what your diary had to say the following morning. (*He reads*) "April nineteenth . . . Liz appears to be over the moon. Never seen such a change overnight! But why is she so intent on listening to the radio? It's most unlike her . . ."

Max She had the radio on the whole time. Even whilst she was typing! I just couldn't understand it.
Digby It never occurred to you that she was listening to the news bulletins?
Max No, I must confess it didn't. But I realize now that it should have done.

Digby nods and closes the diary. He then picks up the gun and puts it in his briefcase

You still haven't answered the question I asked you the first time we met. Why was Terry Wilde interested in my wife?
Digby Wilde knew that both he and his colleagues were being closely watched. You were unknown to the organization and therefore less likely to arouse suspicion. Also, Wilde felt sure that even if they did suspect you, they'd be curious about the clock and waste valuable time examining it. Which is precisely what happened. (*He closes his briefcase and works the combination*)
Max What was the organization aiming to achieve? Or shouldn't I ask that question?
Digby By all means ask it. The media will want to know the answer anyway. They were aiming to destabilize the economic market by assassinating visiting American industrialists and thus cause us embarrassment with our Washington friends.
Max That sounds to me remarkably like the official handout.
Digby (*smiling*) Good. Because that's precisely what it is. (*He picks up his case*) Mr Telligan, forgive my mentioning this, but—if by any chance we bump into each other again, and we might, since like myself I understand you're a frequent visitor to the Tate. Please don't be offended if I fail to recognize you.
Max (*amicably*) I shan't be offended. The chances are I shan't recognize you, Mr Digby. I once cut my daughter dead in a bus queue.
Digby I shall look forward to receiving the same treatment.

Digby nods to Max and exits R

There is a pause, then Max returns, somewhat despondently, to the desk. He sinks into Liz's chair facing the typewriter. For a brief moment he puts his hand on the typewriter, then his eye falls on the copy of the diary. He is staring at the diary, deep in thought, when . . .

Harriet enters from the hall. She stands quietly watching him

Max suddenly looks up

Max (*rising*) Why, hello, Harriet!
Harriet I've brought your key back. Marsha won't be needing it. She's not coming at the weekend.
Max (*moving towards her*) Yes, I know. She telephoned.
Harriet Oh.
Max (*taking the key from her*) The party's off, I take it?
Harriet Yes. I'm glad to say. Well—I won't keep you, Max. I've got a taxi waiting and I'm on my way to the station. (*She moves to go*)

Max (*as she does so*) No, wait a minute! Don't go, Harriet (*He opens a drawer in the desk and takes out a car key*) There's no need for a taxi. You can use the Volvo.
Harriet (*taken aback*) The Volvo?
Max Yes.
Harriet You've bought the Volvo?

Max nods

   Our Volvo?
Max That's right.
Harriet What on earth are you trying to do, Max? Turn the clock back?
Max The garage did that.

Harriet smiles and for a long moment they stand looking at each other

   What are you thinking, Harriet?
Harriet You'll have to do something about the heater.

Max bursts out laughing and is just about to embrace her as——

The CURTAIN falls

FURNITURE AND PROPERTY LIST

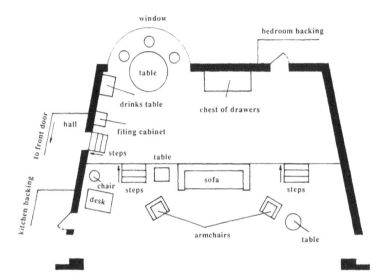

ACT I

SCENE 1

On stage: Armchairs
Sofa. *On it:* cushions
Filing cabinet
Antique chest of drawers
Occasional tables. *On them:* lamps
Desk. *On it:* several unopened letters, dictating machine, typewriter with sheet of paper in it, typing paper, notebook, pens, stiletto-type paper-knife, reference books including BA timetable, lamp, telephone, address/telephone book, folder of papers, box of cigarettes. *Under it:* **Liz**'s handbag
Drinks table. *On it:* decanter (nearly empty), various bottles of drink, glasses, ashtray
Bookcase. *In it:* leather-bound "Max Telligan" novels

Dining-table
Chairs
Carpet
Window curtains (open)
On walls: signed photographs of well-known personalities

Off stage: Copy of *Evening Standard* **(Liz)**
Suitcase, large parcel **(Max)**

Personal: **Harriet:** handbag with Inland Revenue envelope

SCENE 2

Strike: Newspaper
Harriet's handbag
Suitcase, parcel
Paper from typewriter

Set: Kitchen door closed
Folder closed on desk
Liz's handbag on desk
Clock on table
Large carrier bag in desk drawer

Off stage: Valise **(Crane)**
Wallet-style case containing gun **(Lloyd)**

Personal: **Crane:** walking-stick, wallet with CID identity card
Max: key in pocket
Harriet: handbag

SCENE 3

Strike: Case

Set: Gun in locked drawer of filing cabinet

Off stage: Carrier bag with clock **(Crane)**
Suitcase with clothing, slippers, dressing gown, toilet bag, book, calcula-
tor in pocket of jacket **(Max)**
Dark sheet **(Max)**

Personal: **Crane:** walking-stick, blood sac under shirt
Max: filing-cabinet key
Harriet: handbag

SCENE 4

Strike: Sheet
Walking-stick
Suitcase, clothing, etc.
Gun

Set: **Digby**'s briefcase containing small camera, small photograph on desk
Calculator on desk

Off stage: Large manuscript **(Max)**

ACT II

Scene 1

Off stage: Bottle of whisky (**Max**)
            Drink (**Jeff**)
            Drink (**Connie**)
            Blood for face, hands, dress (**Connie**)

Personal: **Harriet:** handbag containing lighter
            Liz: handbag containing card, wrist-watch

Scene 2

Strike: Photograph
            Bottle

Set: Decanter full of whisky
            Kitchen door closed

Off stage: Briefcase containing diary manuscript with markers (**Digby**)

Personal: **Jeff:** cigarette
            Digby: bugging device in pocket

Scene 3

Strike: Briefcase

Set: Receiver on telephone
            Documents/contract on desk

Check: Paper-knife on desk

Off stage: Bunch of cellophane-wrapped flowers (**Liz**)
            Hat, coat (**Max**)
            Short nylon rope (**Jeff**)

Personal: **Liz:** handbag
            Lloyd: packet of cigarettes in pocket

Scene 4

Strike: Rope, knife

Set: Newspapers, various letters, **Liz**'s notebook on desk
            Car key in desk drawer

Off stage: Valise (**Liz**)
            Briefcase containing diary manuscript with markers (**Digby**)

Personal: **Liz:** handbag containing gun
            Harriet: handbag, key

LIGHTING PLOT

Property fittings required: several table lamps

Interior. A living-room. The same scene throughout

ACT I, SCENE 1   Afternoon

To open: General interior lighting

Cue 1	**Max:** ". . . get hold of this story?" *Black-out*	(Page 7)

ACT I, SCENE 2   Late afternoon

To open: General interior lighting

Cue 2	**Max** stares at the gun in astonishment *Black-out*	(Page 19)

ACT I, SCENE 3   Night

To open: General interior lighting, table lamps on

Cue 3	**Harriet** quickly exits *Fade to Black-out*	(Page 26)

ACT I, SCENE 4   Night

To open: General interior lighting, table lamps on

Cue 4	**Max:** "It's my wife." *Fade slowly to Black-out*	(Page 27)

ACT II, SCENE 1   Night

To open: General interior lighting, table lamps on

Cue 5	**Max:** ". . .in the clubhouse." *Fade lights*	(Page 38)
Cue 6	When ready *Bring up lighting on table in alcove*	(Page 38)
Cue 7	**Max** goes, **Connie** continues sitting at the table *Fade lighting on table in alcove*	(Page 41)
Cue 8	When ready *Bring up interior lighting as before*	(Page 41)
Cue 9	**Max** desperately dials for help *Black-out*	(Page 41)

ACT II, SCENE 2   Morning

To open: General interior lighting

Cue 10   **Digby** attaches bugging device to telephone   (Page 49)
            Fade to Black-out

ACT II, SCENE 3   Afternoon

To open: General interior lighting

Cue 11   As **Lloyd** falls to the ground   (Page 53)
            Black-out

ACT II, SCENE 4   Morning

To open: General interior lighting

No cues

EFFECTS PLOT

ACT I

Cue 16	As **Liz** moves towards the hall *Telephone rings*	(Page 36)
Cue 17	**Liz** exits *Repeat Cue 2*	(Page 36)
Cue 18	**Harriet** and **Max** exit into the hall together *Repeat Cue 2*	(Page 42)
Cue 19	**Max** (*on the phone*): "... at the same hotel ..." *Doorbell rings*	(Page 42)
Cue 20	**Max** (*on the phone*): "... spoken to you about him?" *Doorbell rings*	(Page 42)
Cue 21	**Max** goes out into the hall *Repeat Cue 2*	(Page 42)
Cue 22	Sound of disturbance in hall, terrified scream from **Connie** *Front door slams*	(Page 44)
Cue 23	**Max** and **Jeff** exit into hall *Repeat Cue 2*	(Page 46)
Cue 24	**Max** nods and exits *Repect Cue 2*	(Page 50)
Cue 25	**Liz** places sheet of paper in typewriter *Doorbell rings*	(Page 50)
Cue 26	**Liz** goes out into hall *Front door opens*	(Page 50)
Cue 27	**Lloyd:** "... and what I am——" *Telephone rings*	(Page 52)
Cue 28	**Liz** picks up flowers and exits *Repeat Cue 2*	(Page 52)
Cue 29	**Max:** "... which need answering." *Telephone rings*	(Page 55)
Cue 30	**Liz** switches on dictating machine *Voices and effects as script pages 55-56*	(Page 55)
Cue 31	**Digby** nods and exits R *Door opens and closes off*	(Page 58)

MADE AND PRINTED IN GREAT BRITAIN BY
LATIMER TREND & COMPANY LTD PLYMOUTH

MADE IN ENGLAND

Ingram Content Group UK Ltd.
Milton Keynes UK
UKHW031419270423
420877UK00016B/939

9 780573 016929